ACCORDING TO
KATE

ACCORDING TO
KATE

The Legendary Life of Big Nose Kate,
Love of Doc Holliday

CHRIS ENSS

TWODOT®

Helena, Montana
Guilford, Connecticut

A · TWODOT® · BOOK

An imprint and registered trademark of The Rowman & Littlefield Publishing Group, Inc.
4501 Forbes Blvd., Ste. 200
Lanham, MD 20706
www.rowman.com

Distributed by NATIONAL BOOK NETWORK

British Library Cataloguing in Publication Information available

Library of Congress Cataloging-in-Publication Data available

ISBN 978-1-4930-3773-5 (hardcover)
ISBN 978-1-4930-3774-2 (e-book)

∞ The paper used in this publication meets the minimum requirements of American National Standard for Information Sciences—Permanence of Paper for Printed Library Materials, ANSI/NISO Z39.48-1992.

Contents

Acknowledgments

Writing this book has been a lesson in uninterrupted anguish. Kate Elder was a controversial character, quite disliked by one of the most celebrated figures in the Old West. The mere idea that I was going to tackle a nonfiction book about the troubled, soiled dove brought on a barrage of criticism from historians and Earp-family enthusiasts. The following are to blame for my continuing on with the project despite the threats made against writing the book.

Scott Dyke: award-winning journalist and keeper of Kate's personal writings and mementos.

Cathy Reeves: former director of the Dodge City Library and expert on Dodge City history.

Stuart Rosebrook: senior editor at *True West Magazine* and the one who continually reminded me that Kate had a head for business.

Erin Turner: editorial director at TwoDot Books, who agreed to let me pursue Kate's story and kept the goal of a completed book looming large long past the deadline.

INTRODUCTION

KATE ELDER WAS A WORKING GIRL. THROUGHOUT MOST OF HER YOUNG life, she was employed as a soiled dove—a woman of ill fame, a sporting gal, a prostitute. She wasn't alone in that profession; hundreds of women entered the trade in the 1800s. Some felt they had no other option but to become a lady of the evening, and others joined the industry of the fallen, believing they could make a fortune capitalizing on the vices of intrepid cowboys and pioneers.

It was Kate's relationship with John Henry (Doc) Holliday that brought her notoriety and lifted her out of the role as mere courtesan to that of common-law wife to the well-known gambler, gunfighter, and dentist.

Kate's story of her life on the frontier as a soiled dove and her time with one of the West's most recognizable characters has value. She was in her eighties when she dared to recall all that had transpired since leaving Hungary where she was born to the events leading up to the historic gunfight at the O.K. Corral. There are those who insist that because of her age her recollections are faulty and that little of anything she said occurred the way she reported it. I maintain it would be wrong not to share all the eighty-four-year-old Kate had to tell about an adventurous time in history merely because she was an octogenarian. Some of us at fifty-seven can't remember what day it is even though we've checked the calendar upwards of twenty times since starting work. Yet I can vividly recall that during seventh grade music class Pam Green loudly pointed out that I was growing a mustache. (It's important to note here that I'm a woman, so this was extremely detrimental to my self-esteem at the time.)

According to Kate is a biography about the life and times of Kate Elder. She would have written the book herself if a publisher had been willing to pay her handsomely for her tale. Kate believed her story was worth a great deal. No one besides Kate saw it that way. Throughout the book I've used all the information contained in Kate's journals, personal letters, and interviews to tell of her life from her childhood in Hungary to her waning years at a retirement home in Arizona. Where some of her details were ambiguous, I used newspapers and historical documents to corroborate her story.

This book is entitled *According to Kate* because it's exactly what Kate said happened. I didn't debate her recollections of events in the text because it would have interrupted the flow of her thoughts and taken readers out of the moment. Occasionally, I added an endnote to clarify what she meant or to shed light on the circumstances, but I didn't dismantle her telling of what she saw or heard. That subject has been covered by many writers before this book was compiled and no doubt will be the subject of many articles to come.

Kate wrote that she loved Doc. She wanted a life with him. According to Kate, the couple seemed to be on their way to settling down in Las Vegas, New Mexico, when the Earps arrived and disrupted the plans. Kate was annoyed by the intrusion and Wyatt Earp's attempts to persuade Doc to leave Las Vegas and travel with them to Arizona. Understandably, most women would be irritated if influential friends tried to coax their significant other away from their home and the life the pair had created. Wyatt viewed Kate's desire to keep Doc with her in New Mexico as controlling. He was critical of her need to know Doc's plans and saddled her with a name she would never be able to shake. Because of this, Kate held a grudge against Wyatt the rest of her life.

I spent more than two years researching Kate Elder's story. In my attempt to find everything Kate had ever written, I sifted through numerous archives from St. Louis, Missouri, to Bisbee, Arizona, corresponded with her distant relatives, and pored over the letters and journals of people Kate knew from her childhood home in Davenport, Iowa, to Dos Cabezas, Arizona. Award-winning journalist Scott Dyke provided me with the lion's share of Kate Elder's personal writings. The collection included photographs Kate owned and interviews Kate did with Dr. A. W. Bork as well as all the research Dr. Bork did with controversial author Glenn Boyer. Any thought I had that the bulk of the material in the collection hadn't been seen before was quickly dispelled once I began going through it. There were aspects of Kate's life within the collection that had not been made public, but most of what I was given had been shared with other writers. Still, I'm grateful to have been exposed to the artifacts of such an independent and driven woman.

Kate Elder was strong willed. She made as much money as possible as fast as she could, spent it just as quickly, and outlasted most sporting gals of that time. She was known by several names throughout her life. Kate Elder, Kate Fisher, Big-Nose Kate, Mrs. J. H. Holliday, and Mary K. Cummings were a few of the most common titles. According to Kate, "I've been called many things. Some not so kind. I only ever cared what those I loved called me." Not a bad attitude to have as a harlot and critic of Old West royalty. No doubt that's how she survived as long as she did.

CHAPTER ONE

The Girl from Hungary

KATE ELDER SAT ON THE BALCONY OF THE DODGE HOUSE HOTEL IN Dodge City, Kansas, cradling a rifle in her lap. It was a warm night in mid-June 1878. She was wearing a white cotton and lace slip dress that accentuated her curves and did little to cover her other assets. The sound of an inexperienced accordion player squeezing out a tune mixed with the laughter from the patrons in the billiard hall next door filled the night air.[1]

Kate studied a pair of drunken soldiers as they exited the billiard hall, climbed aboard their waiting horses, and rode off in the direction of Fort Dodge, the military post five miles east of town. Once the soldiers were out of sight, she relaxed the hold she had on the gun and rubbed her tired eyes. Kate had too much character in her face to be outright pretty, but she attracted men like flies. At that moment, the only man's affections she cared to attract were John Henry Holliday's, a Georgia dentist and gambler prone to settle disagreements in a violent manner.[2]

An unfortunate incident with the law had made it necessary for Kate and Doc to leave Fort Griffin, Texas, in a hurry and seek refuge in Dodge City. Their abrupt exit from the southwestern cavalry fort had Kate worried the authorities would be searching for them and, when they were found, Doc would be made to return to answer for his wrongdoings. Kate wasn't going to let that happen.[3]

Since arriving in Dodge City in late May 1878, Kate had reacquainted herself with the cow town where she'd lived and worked in 1875.[4] Dodge City was a wild burg that straddled the Santa Fe rails. Cowpunchers found it to be the best place to end a drive. The saloons were endless and

The Dodge House Hotel and Billiard Hall, Dodge City, Kansas, 1874
COURTESY OF KANSAS STATE HISTORICAL SOCIETY

always open. Gamblers found numerous individuals to challenge, sporting women swarmed like bees, and bad men frequently sharpened their aim on citizens. The men behind the badges in Dodge City were well-known western figures. Wyatt Earp, Bat Masterson, and Bill Tilghman all took a turn at maintaining law and order in the trigger-happy town.[5] How Kate Elder, from Pest, Hungary, came to be a fixture in a wide-open town primed with free-flowing money from the cattle trade and inundated by hordes of gunmen, outlaws, rustlers, and ladies of easy virtue was a question Kate pondered on a regular basis.[6]

She shifted the gun in her lap and stared out at the massive night sky and the stars that riddled the great expanse, contemplating a similar sky that hung over the steamer that brought her parents, brothers and sisters, and her from Bremen, Germany, to America when she was ten years old.[7] Kate remembered her life before, when she was filled with hope and the promise of prosperity and success.

This tintype is believed to be an early image of Mary Katharine Horony, aka Kate Elder. CHRIS ENSS

John Henry Holliday when he gradu- ated from dental school in March 1872 CHRIS ENSS

One of seven children, Kate Elder was born Maria Izabella Magdolna on November 7, 1850, in Hungary.* Her father, Mihaly (Michael) Horony, was a German physician.** Her mother, Katalin (Katharina) Baldizar, was a homemaker.*** Michael was able to provide well for his family. He had close ties to Prince Ferdinand Maximilian, younger brother of Austrian emperor Francis Joseph I. Maximilian was named ruler of Mexico by Napoleon III (of France). If not for the revolution that overcame the country, Doctor Horony, undoubtedly serving as Maximilian's personal physician, and his family would have enjoyed a life of plenty in Mexico.[8]

In early 1860 political unrest prompted Doctor Horony to flee Hungary with his wife and children. They boarded a steamer out of Bremen,

---

* The baptismal record from Ersekujvar, Hungary, November 9, 1849, conflicts with family records indicating Kate was born in 1850. Whether the baptismal record or the family record is incorrect is unknown.
** Michael was a professor at a teacher training college in Ersekujvar while he was studying to be a doctor at a medical school in Ersekujvar. By 1859 he was a practicing physician in east Hungary.
*** Also spelled Catharina Baldizar.

According to historians at the Sharlot Hall Museum Library and Archives, this picture is of Mary Katharine Horony (seated) next to her sister Wilhelmina.

Views of the city in Hungary where Kate Elder was born in 1850 CHRIS ENSS

Germany.[9] The port was a major point of embarkation for emigrants during the nineteenth and twentieth centuries.* Millions of inhabitants from Austria, Hungary, and other Central European nations were seeking opportunities or refuge in the New World.[10]

The Horonys settled in Davenport, Iowa, in November 1862 and resided in a modest home on the corner of Western Avenue and Second Street. Doctor Horony resumed his medical practice, tending to the residents in town as well as those men who came to the area to enlist in the army. The doctor's son, Victor, joined the military in 1862. Just before the Civil War began, Davenport was declared to be Iowa's first military headquarters.[11]

Kate and her younger brothers and sisters attended local schools. Many people who lived in Davenport were from Germany and Hungary. The Horony children had no trouble settling in with other students who spoke the same language and were speaking English. For a time, it seemed life in America for the Horonys was good. On November

*From 1832 Bremen port officials kept meticulous records on their ship's passengers. Then, in 1874, the authorities, citing a lack of space, destroyed all Bremen passenger records except for those of the current year and two previous years.

28, 1863, Mary's oldest sister Emelia married attorney Francis Gustav Susemihl. The family attended the wedding and celebrated the good fortune of the eldest female Horony child.[12]

In March 1865 Katharina Baldizar Horony passed away after suffering with typhoid fever. Michael Horony died the following month on April 28 from an unknown ailment. "Dr. Horony, a well-known German physician in this city, died very suddenly yesterday at his residence," the April 29, 1865, edition of *Davenport Daily Gazette* reported. "He was out in his garden attending some plants and all at once, feeling unwell, went into his home, sat down and expired in a very short time."[13]

Michael and Katharina's five minor children went to live with Emelia and Gustav until the will could be read and the Horonys' wishes put into effect. All of Michael and Katharina's belongings, including livestock and household items, were sold at auction and the funds put into an account to be used for the care of Alexander, Louis, Rosalia, Mary, and Wilhelmina. On July 17, 1865, family friend Otto Smith was named administrator of Michael Horony's estate. He assumed responsibility for the five minor children and shortly thereafter Emelia and Gustav left the state

The recreation grounds of the Ursuline Academy in St. Louis. According to Kate, she and her sister Wilhelmina attended the school there. CHRIS ENSS

to travel to Europe. According to the administration papers included in the Horony will and probate records, Otto submitted receipts for "clothing, boarding, and lodging" for Alexander, Louis, and Rosalia only.[14] Kate notes in her memoir that she and Wilhelmina were sent to the Ursuline Convent and Boarding School in St. Louis in early 1866.[15]

The Ursuline Convent and Boarding School was established in 1848. The Sisters who came to labor at the facility were from Austria, Germany, and Hungary. Located on the Mississippi River, St. Louis was ideally situated to become the main base of interregional trade. It was the destination for massive immigration by Irish and Germans. Mary and Wilhelmina were not accustomed to the constant activity St. Louis enjoyed. Mary was fascinated with the number of people around day and night. She was attracted to the music wafting out of the saloons and mesmerized by the happy patrons wandering in and out of the establishments. It was a lifestyle from which she had been sheltered, but one she wanted to know better.[16]

The Ursuline Convent where Mary claimed she and Wilhelmina lived and attended school was located on Illinois Avenue at the corner of Seventh Street. The world within the school and boarding house was considerably more sedate than what Mary had witnessed en route to the facility. The Sisters were kind but protective. A cholera epidemic making its way through the city prompted the Sisters to keep the students quarantined for fear the infection would spread. Sixteen-year-old Mary didn't accept such confinement easily. Historical records at the Ursuline Convent from the 1866 to 1868 time period show that a handful of girls regularly snuck out of their dorms in the evening and were seen at various theaters and public houses. No specific names were recorded, but it wouldn't be difficult to imagine Mary being one of those rebellious young women.[17]

The school year at the Ursuline Convent ran from September to May. During the summer months, the students would return to their homes. Wilhelmina and Mary returned to Davenport to be with their younger siblings. Mary didn't care much for life in Iowa without her parents. She hoped to be able to endure the back and forth from Otto Smith's home to St. Louis until she was old enough to graduate, but at some point decided the situation was impossible and ran away.[18]

Mary Horony made her way to the docks along the Mississippi River. A handful of steamships transporting passengers and freight was anchored along the riverfront. At the location ten years prior, a steamboat captain had deliberately crashed his vessel into a bridge built for the railroad. The structure was the first railroad bridge across the Mississippi, and it threatened the livelihood of steamboat owners and operators. If manufacturers and farmers used the railroad to carry their products out of Iowa, the steamers would be out of work. John Hurd, captain and owner of the steamboat that crashed into the bridge, filed a lawsuit against the Rock Island Railroad Company and demanded the bridge not be rebuilt. Abraham Lincoln was Hurd's lawyer. The Supreme Court ruled against Lincoln and his client and ordered that the bridge be reconstructed.[19]

The steamship business was in a slump for a time but had fully rebounded by the summer of 1867. An eleven-foot ribbon map of the Mississippi River printed in 1866 had brought new trade to the steamship lines. The river was a bulk freight route too. The riverbanks were full of landmarks and tributaries people traveling north and south wanted to see. They also wanted to see the popular towns and cities along the way. St. Louis was one of those cities.[20] When Mary stowed away on one of those steamships, she hoped the vessel would dock at the bustling spot in Missouri.[21]

Stowaways are supposed to keep themselves hidden from the steamship crew, but Mary had a difficult time staying out of sight. Once she was found out, she was taken to the captain of the vessel. Captain Fisher (also Fischer) studied the teenager and the small carpetbag held in her hand then asked her a series of standard questions. Name? From where did you come? Are you in trouble? Are you running from a husband? Mary was evasive at first, but eventually let the captain know a little about her. She told him she was not married and assured him she was in no trouble. He informed her that he wasn't turning the steamer around to take her back to Davenport. The steamer was headed to St. Louis, and it would be several weeks before they returned to the area. Mary didn't object.[22]

It took eight days and seven nights to get to St. Louis. During that time Captain Fisher and Mary became good friends. He shared his experiences as a steamship pilot with her along with tales of tragedies that could occur. The sinking of the steamship *Evening Star* was fresh

Kate found the activity in St. Louis exciting; she made it her home and started her business at this location. CHRIS ENSS

on the minds of many steamship captains and their crew. The *Evening Star* had set sail for New Orleans from New York in September 1866. It encountered a hurricane off the coast of Georgia and sank.[23] Two hundred fifty-three people drowned. Mary listened with wide-eyed interest at the unfortunate story then recounted her own tragic tale of losing her mother and father and of separating from family when some stayed behind in Iowa while others were sent to the Ursuline Convent.[24]

Mary didn't take advantage of the education offered to her at the convent. If she had remained in school, she might have been able to reap the benefits. The Ursuline Sisters hoped to prepare young girls to be governesses and teachers. They wanted the girls to have the opportunities to pursue other areas of work besides that of laundress or cook. The deaths of numerous marriageable men because of the Civil War had left many young, single women in a position to provide for themselves. They would not be able to readily count on a husband to fill that role and an education was essential.[25]

By the time the steamship arrived in St. Louis, Mary and Captain Fisher had forged a strong bond, one that would remain for the rest of her life. When she left the steamer, she began using the name Kate Fisher, after the riverboat pilot who had shown her kindness.[26]

Any ties Mary had to her old life in Davenport, Iowa, were severed in the late 1860s. In 1869 she signed an affidavit naming Otto Smith as her "true and lawful attorney." He had her permission to handle any affairs she might have in Davenport and to give whatever funds might be coming her way from the sale of her parents' property to her siblings. At nineteen, she was planning to make St. Louis her home.[27]

Job opportunities for young women in a place like St. Louis were limited. It was the fourth largest city in the United States. The population exploded in the late 1860s as many emigrants from Germany and Ireland poured into the area. St. Louis was the gateway to the West. It was the chief provisioner and jumping-off point for westward-bound explorers, adventurers, and gold prospectors. The transportation industry was growing, and many who chose to stay in the city either worked for the railroad or steamship lines.[28]

The business of vice was booming too. There were laws against prostitution, but they were largely unenforced as the more urgent demands of lust and money proved irresistible. It was in this line of work that Mary Katherine Horony, now Kate Fisher, decided to venture. Kate never explained why she became a sporting woman. One can only imagine that it would have been at once heartbreaking and astonishing for Doctor Horony and his wife to have thought their daughter could pursue such a profession. Perhaps Kate couldn't find work that suited her personality. Maybe she couldn't find any work that didn't involve cleaning up after someone, or maybe she liked being a soiled dove and belonging to no one man. Money may have been the predominant attraction to the profession. Good money could be earned, but the business was fraught with danger from disease and ambient physical conditions. Marriage might have been another inducement to enter that line of work. Some women met and married businessmen or prospectors on the job. They had families and lived out their days far removed from the profession. Whatever the reason, Kate and the trade would be forever tied.[29]

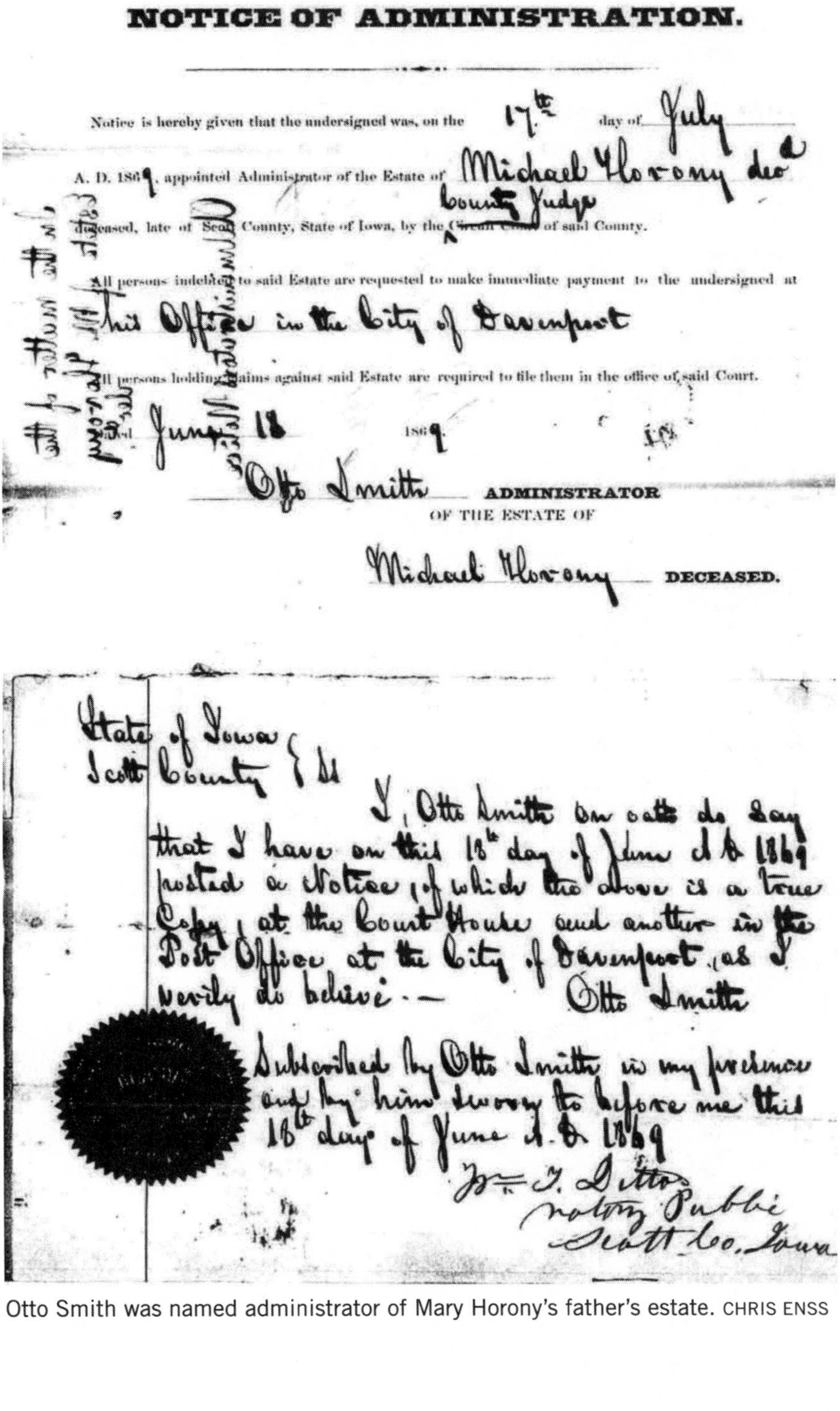

NOTICE OF ADMINISTRATION.

Notice is hereby given that the undersigned was, on the 17ᵗʰ day of *July*

A. D. 186*9*, appointed Administrator of the Estate of *Michael Horony dec*

County Judge

deceased, late of Scott County, State of Iowa, by the Circuit Court of said County.

All persons indebted to said Estate are requested to make immediate payment to the undersigned at

this Office in the City of Davenport

All persons holding claims against said Estate are required to file them in the office of said Court.

Dated *June 18* 186*9*

Otto Smith **ADMINISTRATOR**
OF THE ESTATE OF

Michael Horony **DECEASED.**

State of Iowa
Scott County §§

I, Otto Smith on oath do say that I have on this 18ᵗʰ day of June A D 1869 posted a Notice, of which the above is a true Copy, at the Court House and another in the Post Office at the City of Davenport, as I verily do believe.— *Otto Smith*

Subscribed by Otto Smith in my presence and by him sworn to before me this 18ᵗʰ day of June A D 1869

Wm J. Ditto
notary Public
Scott Co. Iowa

Otto Smith was named administrator of Mary Horony's father's estate. CHRIS ENSS

According to Kate, it was during this time when she was establishing herself in business in St. Louis that she met and married a dentist named Silas Melvin. United States census records from that time period list two men named Silas Melvin. One was married to a steamship captain's daughter and the other was an attendant at an asylum.* Kate claimed she and Silas married and moved to Georgia.[30]

Kate was in her eighties when she sat down with Southern Illinois University professor Dr. A. W. Bork to share the story of her life. She might have confused Silas with a man she had yet to meet. He was a dentist from Georgia, and the impact he had on her cast a shadow over all her memories.[31] There is no record of her union with Silas Melvin. Historians speculate Melvin might have been a regular caller at the start of her career as a prostitute.[32]

It's likely that Kate worked in a brothel as opposed to the streets. In 1870 the city of St. Louis passed a "social evil ordinance" which allowed prostitution so long as it was conducted in a brothel instead of on the streets. The July 31, 1870, edition of the *Chicago Tribune* reported on the unusual regulation. "Assuming that the vice of licentiousness cannot be suppressed, that it is inevitable, ineradicable, and absolute concomitant of human society," the article read, "the Common Council of the city has decided to tolerate it, to recognize it as a business, as they do the liquor traffic, and to hedge it about, and throw around the restraints and sanction of the law." Police throughout St. Louis made lists of all the houses of ill repute and the lewd women they could find. Any who opposed registering as a sporting woman were fined twenty dollars.[33]

There are no arrest records that show Kate Fisher was ever fined. The 1870 St. Louis census does list Kate Fisher as a resident of the city and notes her profession as prostitute.[34]

To prevent disease, molestation, taxation, or the disclosure of names to authorities, the social evil ordinance was put into effect to protect men whose vices supported bawdy houses. The responsibility to support the

---

* Coincidentally, Kate occasionally claimed she was the daughter of a steamship captain. She was referring to Captain Fisher being her father.

hospital that dealt with men who "suffered any ailment as a victim of their lust" fell on the women who ran sporting houses and their employees.[35]

If Kate entered the profession because she felt her options were limited as an orphan and a woman, she stayed in the business after learning the power the line of work afforded. Prostitutes could be successful in wild, lawless, and thoroughly renegade boomtowns. By far, they made the highest wages of American women. A sporting girl working for a madam was generally provided with free health care. Also, at a time when women were being told they could not and should not protect themselves from violence and wives had no legal recourse against being raped by their husbands, law enforcement agents were employed by madams to protect the women who worked for them. Many working girls and madams owned and knew how to use guns as well. Most women had no legal right to own property, but successful prostitutes could own land and real estate. Unlike other women, soiled doves could travel because they weren't bound solely to the locations their husbands or fathers moved them to. Where gambling and public drinking were forbidden by most women, prostitutes were fixtures in western saloons and became some of the most successful gamblers in the nation. Madams, those women who owned, managed, and maintained brothels, were generally the only women who appeared to be in control of their own destinies. For a woman like Kate, whose life after her parents died had been directed by two different guardians, the idea of being able to determine her own fate must have been compelling.[36]

The lifestyle, however, wasn't without its dangers. Entertaining numerous men often resulted in assault, unwanted pregnancies, and even death. Some prostitutes escaped the hell of the trade by committing suicide. Some drank themselves to death, and others overdosed on laudanum. Botched abortions, syphilis, and other venereal diseases claimed many lives as well.[37]

Fallen women like Kate learned to live with the negative social stigma associated with their trade. They survived the rough, lawless men in their company and the gossip of "God fearing" women and strongly defended themselves whenever the occasion arose. If by chance they met a kind, generous man who expressed an interest in being with them beyond the evening they had paid for, they often leapt at the chance to try their hand at respectable life.[38]

Kate claimed that Silas promised her happiness, security, a home, and a family. The couple traveled to Atlanta to start their life together. People from virtually every state and many foreign countries were flocking to the rapidly expanding center of the southeast as it continued to recover from the Civil War. Silas believed the pair would prosper in Georgia. Within the first year of marriage, Kate and Silas had a son, and for a moment the young woman from Hungary was happier than she had ever been. Her joy didn't last, however. Both her husband and baby contracted yellow fever and died. Alone again, Kate returned to Missouri and to the profession she knew. Her plan was to forget what she lost, to surround herself with men who knew about the law of restraint, to relish being indifferent to public opinion, to celebrate being unburdened by family, and to drink whenever she felt like it.[39]

CHAPTER TWO

Soiled Dove in a Cow Town

IN THE WINTER OF 1872, WENDELL PHILLIPS, ORATOR, ATTORNEY, AND the soul of John Brown marching on, delivered a lecture to a large audience of concerned citizens in St. Louis, Missouri, about the social cancer that plagued society. He pounded the lectern he stood behind while addressing the crowd and advised them to take a stand against intemperance, crime, and prostitution. Phillips was appalled that city officials had legalized the profession and were issuing licenses to the owners of houses of ill repute and the bawdy women who worked there. Almond Street, a popular thoroughfare five blocks west of the riverfront, was the location of many of those houses. It was Phillips's hope that after the residents of St. Louis heard his fiery speech they would demand the businesses be closed.[1]

"The root of this vice is poverty," Phillips proclaimed. "It is because the poverty of a certain class makes them the victims of the wealth and leisure of another. Give one hundred men anywhere an honest career and a chance at the grand opportunities of life, and ninety out of the hundred will distain to steal. Give one hundred women a fair chance at the grand opportunities that their brothers have and ninety out of the hundred will disdain to barter virtue for gold."[2]

Mary Katherine Horony, now known as Kate Fisher, was one of those near Almond Street who bartered virtue for gold. Poverty had played a part in her decision to become a sporting woman, but she was satisfied the work possessed possibilities beyond money. Kate was a business woman—nothing more, nothing less.[3]

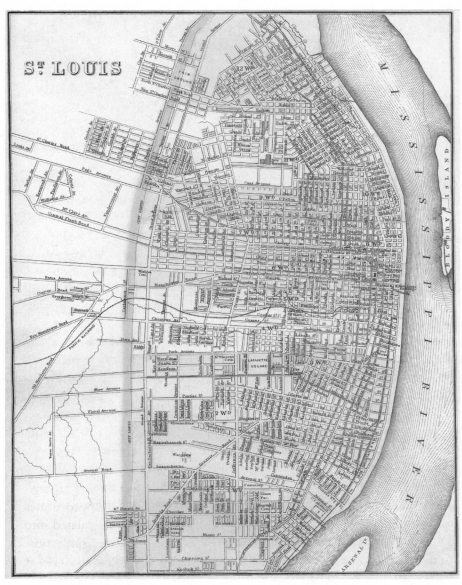

Map of the area in St. Louis where Kate lived and worked in 1872 CHRIS ENSS

St. Louis had given Kate and other sporting women the opportunity to do their job without fear that law enforcement would interfere. The "social evil ordinance" the city had passed in March 1870 not only required prostitutes to obtain licenses but also mandated businesswomen to submit to medical exams testing for venereal diseases. Civic leaders hoped the controversial ordinance would ultimately reduce the spread of disease. Many opposed the idea, arguing that it "encouraged the very vice which all good men and women destined to see suppressed."[4] Many soiled doves never bothered to register. Kate was one of those women.

The spirited Hungarian woman must have been able to take care of herself against intoxicated and belligerent clients. Prostitutes sometimes found themselves in the company of men who resented their services. They hated themselves for hiring sporting women and blamed those women for the ills of society.[5] A listing of arrests in daily St. Louis papers showed how many acts of violence against prostitutes occurred nightly. The August 29, 1872, edition of *the Macon Republican* contained information about the circumstances surrounding the beating deaths of more than ten bawdy ladies in the area of Popular Street in St. Louis.[6]

"Eleven wretched criminals victimized prostitutes overnight," *the Macon Republican* article began. "A man named Burklin shot a sinful woman when crazed with drink and jealousy; another killed a woman with a grubbing hoe; a third tossed the prostitute out a third story window; three were stabbed to death; the seventh prostitute was beaten to death with a soda water bottle; two were strangled; two were hanged by the neck with a rope."[7]

Soiled doves not only ran the risk of losing their lives at the hand of a client, but their coworkers could be a threat too. According to the February 6, 1872, edition of the *St. Louis Weekly Democrat*, a pair of prostitutes got into a fight at Lillie Allen's house and the altercation escalated into a hair-pulling contest. One of the women later died of a scalp infection. There are no records that indicate Kate ever had such issues with any of the other sporting women with whom she shared a house.[8] It's likely in the early days of her career Kate limited time with the other ladies to avoid such difficulties. That wouldn't always be the case.

A depiction of prostitution on Almond Street in
St. Louis in the 1870s CHRIS ENSS

In March 1872, editors with the New York paper *The Observer* sent reporters to major cities from Boston to Denver to do a story on the issue of prostitution. While in St. Louis, reporters surmised there were more than nine hundred prostitutes living and working there. Kate was among those harlots counted.[9] When all the calculations were concluded, it was determined that there were as many prostitutes in the country as there were soldiers in the United States Army during the height of the Civil War.[10]

The area in every city where sporting women were located was referred to as the red-light district. The origin of the term came about because railroad men left their red signal lanterns outside the brothels while paying a visit to a lady of the evening. They did that so they could be found in an emergency. The sign of a red lantern on the porch eventually became known as a way to identify brothels that often appeared as legitimate homes and businesses on the outside. Many red-light districts got their start alongside railroad tracks where numerous saloons already stood. Railroad employees and visitors alike could stop for a pleasure visit.

Kate's place of business was not only located near railroad tracks but also close to the waterfront where steamships were docked, and crew members were free to visit bawdy houses close by.[11] There was always more than enough work for Kate and the other soiled doves in town.

Among the men Kate spent time with in 1872 was a twenty-year-old man named John Henry (Doc) Holliday. The Georgia native had recently graduated from the Pennsylvania College of Dental Surgery and had traveled to St. Louis to join a classmate at his practice. The classmate's name was A. Jameson Fuches Jr. Fuches had an office on Fourth Street. According to a transcript of Kate's recollections taken down by author and actor Anton Mazzanovich, "Doc Holliday was born of Scotch-Irish parents in Atlanta, Georgia. His mother died when he was born, and he was raised by his grandmother. When John finished his schooling, his father took him to Philadelphia and placed him in a college to study dentistry. His father died while he was in college. After graduation he stayed in Philadelphia for a while, then went to St. Louis, where he opened an office near the Planter's Hotel on Fourth Street."[12]

Doc Holliday was actually born in Griffin, Georgia. His father was a lawyer, planter, local politician, and major in the Confederate Army. His mother was remembered for her beauty and musical talent. Doc was known for his excellent manners and courtly air and for his youthful enthusiasm for riding and shooting. He had a strong commitment to his profession but was restless and high strung with an appetite for excitement.[13] According to Kate, "Doc was close to six feet tall, weight one hundred and sixty pounds, fair complexion, very pretty mustache, a blonde, blue-grey eyes, and a fine set of teeth."[14]

Kate enjoyed the time she spent with Doc, but if she imagined he would decide to propose and stay in Missouri, she was woefully wrong. Doc had every intention of returning to Georgia and building a dental practice with his cousin Robert Alexander Holliday.[15] In July 1872 Doc did indeed return to the place of his birth, and Kate records she was with him when he went back to Georgia. According to her, the pair had just married when Doc received a letter from his grandmother in Atlanta asking him to come home.*[16]

* In some places in Kate's memoir she indicated that she and Doc married in 1876.

John Henry (Doc) Holliday

"So, we went to Georgia," she told author Anton Mazzanovich, "and several months after we arrived in that city his grandmother died. Her estate had been willed to her grandson, John H. Holliday, with a provision that two thousand dollars be given to [family friend] who had been with the family for many years. It took three months to settle the estate according to the provisions of the will, which amounted to $10,000, my husband received $8,000."[17]

Historians such as Gary Roberts note that Doc did return to Georgia to claim an inheritance, but explained the inheritance was from John's mother and not his grandmother.[18] There are no documents available to verify that Kate and Doc were ever legally married.

Both Kate and Doc decided to go West at roughly the same time. Doc had been diagnosed with tuberculosis and headed West primarily for health reasons.[19] He ended up in Texas. Kate got as far as Wichita. The reason the two went their separate ways is not included in Kate's reminiscences.

Wichita, Kansas, in the early 1870s was a thriving cow town filled with a motley array of people scrambling to make a living along the Little Arkansas River. Prior to its becoming a frontier trading post in 1864, the Osage Indians had gathered on the location. The surrounding country was abundant in game, water, and grasses. By the time Kate Fisher moved to town the Osage were no longer around, and the main thoroughfare was a steady stream of cattle, cowboys, wagons, and horses. At night the dance halls came alive; painted courtesans paraded up and down the wooden walkways lining the streets, and drunken brawls were the norm along with sounds of fighting, yelling, swearing, and the ring of revolvers. The Atchison, Topeka, and Santa Fe Railroad passed through the busy region, adding another layer to the chaos. There was some semblance of refinements of civilization there such as a real police department, a functioning legal system, stone commercial block buildings, churches, banks, and schools. Catering to the desires of the young single cowboys and frontier men, an enterprising young woman could make a good living for herself in such an environment. Kate joined the ranks of those young women.[20]

Sporting women in cow towns made the bulk of their money from April or May, when the cattle-shipping season was beginning, to September when it concluded. Although prostitution was made illegal when Wichita was incorporated in 1870, little attempt was made to suppress the trade. The general aim of anti-prostitution ordinances was to financially support the city government and the police force through fines paid to the city.[21]

An anti-prostitution ordinance was signed into effect on August 10, 1871, and, according to the *Wichita Daily Eagle*, the ordinance "provided for the arrest and fine of all persons engaged in gambling and prostitution." The city was running heavily in debt due to the need to maintain a strong police force. "The ordinary revenues of the city were not adequate," the report read. "It is wise and proper that the class who entail this additional expense should meet it with their own contributions, and thus afford themselves protection under the wings of the law. We do not stop to inquire whether anything better could be done. We consider any form of vice under restrictions of the law in some manner within the bounds of mutual protection. Its eradication is not a question. Where the carrion is there you will find the buzzard. The fines are extended to the houses of ill-fame and those who inhabit them."[22]

Kate Fisher was an inhabitant of a house of ill fame run by James Earp's wife, Nellie "Bessie" Ketchum.*[23] Born in New York in 1840, Bessie was a prostitute turned madam. James, a saloonkeeper, and Bessie married in April 1873. Both Bessie and Kate had difficulties with the law in Wichita. Police court records show that the general procedure for collecting fines was that the city marshal would arrest prostitutes on approximately a monthly basis and escort them to the police court where they routinely paid the minimal fine for being an "inmate" or a "keeper" of a house of ill fame. They were then generally not arrested by the police until the next month. In some cases, prostitutes were even arrested on the same day every month, an indication of the "licensing" nature of this procedure.[24]

The May 28, 1873, edition of the *Wichita Daily Eagle* reported that fines paid by prostitutes and saloon owners brought in thousands of dollars. Prostitutes were fined ten dollars, and madams were fined twenty

*James Earp was Wyatt Earp's oldest brother.

dollars.[25] In June 1874 Kate was arrested for working at a "sporting house" and paid a ten-dollar fine. She was arrested again on the same charge in August 1874. The arrest record listed her last name as "Earb." No doubt, law enforcement officials associated Kate with the owners of the house where she worked.[26] Kate's employers were arrested again on September 12, 1874, for operating a house of ill repute. The case against Bessie Earp was dismissed on September 15 after the madam paid a hefty fine.[27]

The fines collected from Kate and other soiled doves like her in Wichita in 1873 and 1874 were large enough to make the levying of general business taxes, common in other frontier towns at the time, unnecessary.[28]

The respectable ladies of Wichita did not approve of Kate, her profession, or the other harlots in the community. They resented law enforcement and city officials' tolerance of prostitution. In the spring of 1874, they submitted to the city council a petition signed by seventy-four local women asking to suppress all houses of ill repute. The petition read as follows:[29]

"To the Mayor and City Council of Wichita, the undersigned citizens of the city of Wichita do most respectfully but earnestly petition your Honorable body, that you take such steps as may be necessary of expedience for the enforcement of the ordinances of the city relating to bawdy houses and houses of ill fame; and that such houses now in existence in our city may be suppressed, and the inmates of the same dealt with according to the law. And we pray that if in the opinion of your city attorney the ordinances now on record are insufficient to carry into effect the intention of the law under which our city is organized, that proper and sufficient ordinances to that end may be immediately passed and rigidly enforced."[30]

Kate and the rest of the harlots at the Earps' house of ill repute were confident that city officials (some of whom spent time at the business) would not act on the petition. Articles in the *Wichita Weekly Eagle* echoed the courtesans' belief but added that "respectability and changing moral sentiment would eventually overtake the town." The June 8, 1874, edition of the *Wichita Weekly Eagle* reported that "Wichita is fast getting rid of prostitutes, cowboys, and gamblers—the elements which has proven such

Main Street and Douglas Street, Wichita, Kansas, 1873 COURTESY OF KANSAS STATE
HISTORICAL SOCIETY

a curse to her prosperity, thanks to the county attorney and the improved
sentiment of the place which is backing him up."[31]

The war against the soiled doves launched by the decent people of
society combined with the changes being made in the cattle industry
prompted Kate to consider moving from Wichita. By the mid-1870s, settlers were fencing off the prairie and the Chisholm Trail with barbed wire,
and many cattle drives shifted west to Dodge City. Kate decided to follow
the cattle drives to Dodge. She was a businesswoman who could foresee
that cowhands would soon overrun the town and that her chance to make
more money had shifted west too. Prior to moving to Dodge City, she
spent time in another popular Kansas cattle town known as Great Bend.[32]

Located at the "great bend" in the Arkansas River where its course
turns eastward, the town was a hub of activity when the Atchison,
Topeka, and Santa Fe Railroad reached the area and it became a shipping point for cattle.[33] Shortly after Kate arrived in Great Bend, she took

a job working for a saloonkeeper named J. S. Elder. Elder was an affable man with numerous friends. He liked fine cigars and white wine made from Catawba grapes, both of which he served in abundance at his establishment. Kate must have found J. S.'s personality pleasing because she adopted his name after she had been working for him for a short time. Kate's job was to entertain the saloon patrons, first by selling them as much as they could drink and then spending the evening with them.[34]

An incident involving Elder's business, and more than likely Kate, was covered in the August 20, 1874, edition of the *Great Bend Register*. The comical episode, which occurred on August 18, 1874, involved a Ford County attorney named Henderson. While attending court in town, Henderson spent his evenings frequenting watering holes. One of those watering holes was J. S. Elder's. Henderson enjoyed buying rounds of drinks for the bar, and all those present happily accepted. Henderson overindulged one night and just before passing out bragged to everyone about the importance of his job as county attorney. While passed out from his intoxicating state, the women in Elder's employ (including Kate) painted the lawyer's face "a la Indian warrior." Henderson was unaware his face had been painted when he came to and proceeded out the saloon. The residents of Great Bend shared a hearty laugh at the sight of the self-important lawyer parading through town looking like he was readying to go into battle on the plains.[35]

Businessman Tom Sherman submitted a report on the incident for the *Great Bend Register*. Sherman would later go into business with Elder and operate similar saloons in Dodge City and Mobeetie, Texas. Sherman was the exact opposite of Elder. He was a lame, oversized man who never shied away from a fight. Sherman and Elder's partnership was short-lived.[36]

The time Kate spent in Great Bend wasn't strictly made up of all amusing, drunken pranks. On November 1874 the soiled dove found herself in trouble with the law again. She was arrested for assault and battery and fined ten dollars. Kate's fine and the ones paid by other women in her profession in Great Bend in 1874 totaled more than $2,440. Soiled doves paid more than 40 percent of the city's budget in the burgeoning cow town that year. Kate was aware of the contribution

Main Street in Great Bend, Kansas, 1870-1880
COURTESY OF KANSAS STATE HISTORICAL SOCIETY

she made providing capital to keep Great Bend and towns like it running. Knowing that fact took the edge off being treated as an outcast by the morally superior ladies in various communities. What she did for a living brought about civil order of sorts, the likes of which nonworking women could not achieve.[37]

J. S. Elder made frequent trips to Dodge City and shared tales of the activity there with Kate. The town, now recognized as the Cowboy Capital, metropolis of the Southwest, and the division point on the Santa Fe Railroad, was visited by many celebrities. Elder was at the Long Branch Saloon in June 1874 when President Grant stopped to pay a call on city leaders. Elder described Dodge as the perfect location for a business-woman like Kate. Lured by the possibility of earning more money in a town with a reputation not only for famous visitors but also debauchery of every kind, Kate left Great Bend for Dodge City. She told few people of her plans, least of all the post office, which as of late November 1874 was still holding mail addressed to her in Great Bend. Kate and J. S. Elder parted company en route to the cattle town. Kate continued to Dodge City.[38]

According to the census taken on March 1, 1875, Kate was a resident of Dodge City at the age of twenty-four.[39] Kate went to work at one of Dodge's earliest saloons—a place called Sherman's. It was owned and operated by Tom Sherman and Charles Norton, a wholesale liquor dealer and businessman. The watering hole stood south of the railroad tracks and north of the Santa Fe Trail. Kate performed a variety of jobs at Sherman's Dance Hall and Saloon. In addition to working as a soiled dove, she performed with a group of other sporting women employed at the establishment. The act was billed as the Seven Jolly Sisters. Kate and her coworkers didn't dance so much as they strolled to music across a makeshift stage. The women would parade about several times in the evening, enticing patrons to buy drinks for themselves and those around them. Kate and the others earned a portion of funds made from the alcohol sold.[40]

Front Street in Dodge City, Kansas COURTESY OF KANSAS STATE HISTORICAL SOCIETY

At the end of the night, the atmosphere at Sherman's was rowdy. Sherman's had a reputation for being a volatile establishment. Kate, no doubt, witnessed plenty of brawls and gunfights. One such disagreement occurred on August 5, 1875. According to the August 14, 1875, edition of the *Weekly Atchison Champion,* Mike Sweeny, the county clerk of Ford County, was shot by Tom Sherman. Sweeny went on a drinking spree while he was at Sherman's saloon and got into a fight with the owner of the establishment. "It is supposed the wound will be fatal," the *Champion* reported. "It is not necessary for the country to go into mourning, as there are plenty of better men left."[41]

Kate could discuss the violent happenings at the saloon with fellow harlot Mollie Brennan. Mollie danced alongside Kate as a member of the Seven Jolly Sisters. Occasionally, the pair would venture outside for a walk. Early one afternoon on October 2, the women happened upon the body of a man stretched out on the walkway. The army uniform he was wearing was disheveled; his face was bloody, and he was covered head to foot in mud. A few steps farther was a "bullwhacker"* in the same condition. Kate recognized the bullwhacker as someone she had entertained the previous evening. The women made a few inquiries and learned there had been a fight in town between the soldiers and cowboys after the soldiers left Sherman's Dance Hall. Mollie and Kate continued their stroll and found more soldiers and cowboys lying about in the same conditions. Neither of the women were taken aback by the sight. Working in the professions they did, they had witnessed similar scenes before.[42]

Dodge City was a place of significant trade and was a great outfitting post for freighters and buffalo hunters. Here civilization ceased, and the wild romance and freedom of the plains began. The businessmen of Dodge City didn't want the country overrun with farmers, and they very frankly told them so. They opposed every movement made in that direction on the grounds that it would ruin their trade. They charged farmers twenty-five cents a glass for beer, and equally high, in proportion, for everything else.[43]

Soldiers and bullwhackers fostered equal animosity toward one another. Bullwhackers resented the military's presence on the plains

*A bullwhacker was someone who drove a freight wagon.

because they believed they could protect themselves from hostile Indians and highwaymen. Whenever the two groups were in the same proximity in Dodge City a fight ensued. Sherman's Dance Hall and Saloon, as well as other such establishments, was assured the evening would end in violence if catering to members of both professions at the same time. If they weren't careful, sporting women could be caught by a stray bullet if their disagreement resulted in gunfire.[44]

When business was slow, Tom Sherman would escort Kate and the other sporting women to Fort Dodge. The group would quietly slip into the camp at night and entertain the soldiers. This practice was commonplace—not just for Sherman but other like businesses. It wasn't until March 1879 that a notice banning wagons containing prostitutes from being driven through the fort was issued from the head of the garrison.[45]

Fallen frails like Kate Elder, who thrived in the business, were much more resilient than the euphemism implied. They had to be tough enough to handle aggressive patrons who could injure them as well as hold their own against combative colleagues who felt they were being cheated out of work.[46] Kate's arrest for assault in 1874 proved she could take care of herself. An incident that occurred in April 1875 was another example of her ability to defend herself. According to Kate and an article in the April 9, 1875, edition of the *Atchison Daily Champion*, a pair of "Demi Monde's" visiting the area got themselves mixed up in a brawl between two owners of houses of ill repute. Kate was having tea at the Eighth Street house with a soiled dove she knew from St. Louis when the madam of the Hotel de Kingston challenged Kate's friend to a fight. Punches were exchanged, and hair was pulled; Kate interjected herself into the situation when she saw that her friend needed help. During the altercation, each filled the air with epithets and curses that would have made a cowboy stare. Citizens pulled the women apart and stopped the brawl. "When they were finally separated, blood was flowing freely from sundry little scratches," the *Atchison Champion* read, "and the battleground was covered with hair. It was a beautiful sight to see the ladies gathering up the trophies of war and starting for their domiciles, their ambitions satisfied and heads swelled."[47]

Between 1875 and 1876 more than 250,000 head of cattle were driven to Dodge along the western trail. The city swelled with cowhands during

Barracks at Fort Dodge, Kansas, 1865-1867
COURTESY OF KANSAS STATE HISTORICAL SOCIETY

spring and summer months. Kate and the other fast girls at Sherman's Dance Hall and Saloon seldom lacked for customers during that time. In August 1875 the same anti-prostitution rhetoric Kate had become familiar with in Wichita was now rearing its head in other Kansas towns. In Atchison, Kansas, citizens were taking steps toward driving out the houses of ill repute there. The public referred to the women who worked in the trade as "daughters of sin" and noted they were a disgrace to the city. There were laws on the books to suppress houses of ill fame, and residents of Atchison demanded appointed officers "enforce the law and shut said houses down." City leaders assured residents they would honor the demand and further stated the desire to force cities throughout the state to comply. "We'll never be rid of this profession unless we address entirely, across the region, the issue in cow towns," council members in Atchison announced.[48]

Civic leaders in Wichita had voiced the same concerns and goals when Kate was working there. "Wichita is a godless hole," an article in the July 15, 1874, edition of the *Wichita Daily Eagle* read. "Prostitution and gambling thrive here, and we must put a stop to the debauchery. . . . Wichita is a bustling, growing place, and some day it will be purified of these coarser elements and take rank as a flourishing town."[49]

At the time Dodge City leaders and politicians in other cow towns were seriously discussing an end to the trade in Kansas, Kate Elder was turning twenty-four. She had been a soiled dove for more than four years.

It was inconceivable to her that prostitution would ever be done away with. Anyone could see that gambling halls and dance houses across the plains were as open as dry-goods stores and hotels, inviting the people to patronize. The headquarters of the cattle trade and the occasional rendezvous of drovers and cowboys, who were for months out upon the plains away from aggregations of humanity, let alone civilization, who, flush with money, were seeking a good time, would always need soiled doves. Kate believed her services would constantly be in demand. The only question was which headquarters of cattle trade would bring the most business.[50]

Tom Sherman, who was as eager to capitalize on the loneliness of cowhands as Kate, decided Sweetwater, Texas, would produce more business for his girls. After driving their livestock through the dry plains on the way to market, cowhands routinely drove their livestock through the area to water the animals along the Brazos River. Sherman decided to take his troupe of dance hall girls to the area to perform for the drovers. Kate Elder was anxious to get away from Dodge City and talk of her livelihood becoming obsolete. She would return to Dodge City some time later with an ailing dentist by her side and a host of gunfighters at her back.[51]

CHAPTER THREE

Riding with Doc Holliday

THE MAIN THOROUGHFARE OF SWEETWATER, TEXAS, WAS SO CROWDED with hunters, trappers, wagons, teams of horses, and soldiers that passing streams of people jostled each other, and some walked shoulder to shoulder.* The air was charged with excitement. Rumors that Tom Sherman, Kate Elder, Mollie Brennan, and the other five members of the Seven Jolly Sisters were on their way had caused a mild panic, and lonely men desperate for female companionship had flocked to the burg.[1]

Sweetwater was a trading post along the Jones Plummer Trail. That trail was connected to the major cattle-drive town of Dodge City. Sweetwater was a destination for bullwhackers, buffalo skinners, and cowhands. Troops from Fort Elliott, eleven miles from town, enjoyed time at Sweetwater too. The fort was established, in 1875, to protect the buffalo traders from being raided by Indians.[2]

For Kate, the busy town provided a fresh crush of people to meet and with whom to do business. Soiled doves relished a change of scenery from time to time. They liked the possibility of enticing new patrons in a different location. It also brought renewed business when sporting girls returned to the town where their house of ill repute was located.[3]

The August 24, 1876, edition of the *Dodge City Times* described the setting where Kate and the other entertainers arrived as a "thriving hamlet overrun with tradesmen." Fourteen wagonloads of buffalo hides for a general outfitter in Dodge City known as Chas. Rath & Co. lined the sides of the dusty roadways. A report that a band of twenty-one hundred

---

*Sweetwater was later named Mobeetie, a Native American word for Sweetwater.

Street Scene, Sweetwater, Texas COURTESY OF SWEETWATER PIONEER MUSEUM

Indians south of Sweetwater had been spotted rattled some of the citizenry, but as long as the soldiers remained in town, panic was abated.[4]

Tom Sherman and his help erected a canvas tent, set up a makeshift stage, and the Seven Jolly Sisters went to work. Among the many individuals who spent time with Sherman's employees was a twenty-three-year-old buffalo hunter and army scout named Bat Masterson. In late 1875 Bat had taken a job as a faro dealer at the Lady Gay Saloon. After Sherman's outfit arrived, Bat could either be found in the saloon or with Mollie Brennan.[5]

On January 24, 1876, Kate and Mollie concluded their dance routine and set off to explore additional business. They ventured to the Lady Gay for a drink. The two ladies met Bat at the bar, and he bought them a drink. Once their drinks were finished, Bat and Mollie retired to his room. Kate recalled the couple hadn't been gone long when Sgt. Melvin A. King, one of the men with whom Bat had been playing cards earlier in the evening, charged toward Bat's room. King was furious with Bat over what he perceived as "underhanded dealings." With a loaded gun in hand, King pounded on Bat's room door and waited for an answer. Assuming it was Kate wanting to join the pair for a nightcap, Bat unlocked the door. Sgt. King burst into the room and opened fire. Mollie came between Bat and one of the bullets and was critically wounded. Bat was shot in the pelvis, but he managed to grab his gun and kill King before collapsing.[6]

Despite his best efforts, the local physician could not save Mollie. An army surgeon was called to the scene to remove the bullet from Bat's lower midsection and stayed with him until he recovered.[7]

Seeking to escape the unpleasantness in Sweetwater, Tom Sherman and his troupe left the area and headed for a town in Shackelford County, Texas, called Fort Griffin. Established in 1867, Fort Griffin was referred to as the heart and soul of the lustiest frontier America has ever known. Situated in the center of Comanche country atop a hill sixteen miles north of Albany, it overlooked the Clear Fork of the Brazos River. Fort Griffin was the last post to be established in west Texas for frontier protection.[8]

Law-abiding ranchers and farmers settled around the post along with gamblers, outlaws, and gunfighters. The settlement down the hill from the camp, known as The Flat, had a reputation for debauchery and unruliness. Just two years prior to Kate Elder and the other soiled doves in Sherman's employ arriving in Fort Griffin, the commander of the post had placed the town, referred to as "Babylon of the Brazos," under martial law. Undesirable elements were asked to leave. The order didn't hold, and little by little bad men and women filtered back into the area.[9]

Business was good for Sherman and his girls. Cowboys, buffalo hunters, and soldiers from the nearby post kept them busy. Between July and November 1876, more than 108,000 cattle and their drovers passed through Fort Griffin.[10] Kate, who was quite popular with those that passed through, entertained six nights a week. Her attitude about being a prostitute was the same as another well-known sporting woman of the time, Denver's Mattie Silks. "I went into the sporting life for business reasons and for no other," Mattie noted. "It was a way to make money, and I made it."[11]

Among the other businesswomen in town earning a living off the cattlemen and hunters was a lady gambler named Carlotta J. Tompkins, also known as Lottie Deno. Lottie was a thirty-year-old lissome auburn-haired woman who was a cold-blooded magician with cards. The men she knew she faced across the green-felted poker tables.[12]

Employed by the Bee Hive Saloon, Lottie was gifted in the art of faro, roulette, and casino. In September 1877 Doc Holliday arrived on the scene and squared off against Lottie at the faro table. Legend has it that Lottie won more than $3,000 from Doc in one game. Legend also has it that Kate Elder suspected Lottie of being interested in Doc beyond card playing. Kate confronted the accomplished gambler about her suspicions, and a yelling match ensued. "Why you low-down, slinkin' slut!" Lottie responded to the accusation. "If I should step in soft cow manure, I would not even clean my boots on that bastard!" Kate was outraged and threatened the lady gambler with a gun she removed from her handbag. Doc stepped in and diffused the situation before any blood was spilled.[13]

Kate makes no mention of Lottie in her memoir. She does write about how happy she was to see Doc again in Fort Griffin. Since his encounter with Kate in Missouri, Doc had been diagnosed with pulmonary tuberculosis, an infectious bacterial disease characterized by the growth of nodules (tubercles) in the tissues, especially the lungs. He had a persistent cough and was painfully thin. He had traveled west to improve his health. He had gambled, drunk, and run afoul of the law since his time as a dental apprentice in St. Louis. Kate was charmed by John but found him to be moody and cynical, especially when he was drinking. An author, historian, and descendant of Doc Holliday, Karen Holliday Tanner, noted in her book *Doc Holliday: A Family Portrait* that Kate was a worldly woman that Doc found to be his "intellectual equal." Kate was strong and independent, and those qualities were attractive to Doc. "She, in turn, liked having an intelligent man with a proper upbringing and mannerly ways. It was in marked contrast to the raucous, rough, unshaven, and crude men who were found in most cattle towns," Holliday Tanner added.[14]

The pair spent a great deal of time together while in Fort Griffin. By day he practiced dentistry, and in the evenings he dealt cards at John Shanssey's Cattle Exchange Saloon. If Kate wasn't working, she was with Doc. She tolerated his occasional angry outbursts and crude remarks, which he confessed ran counter to the well-mannered way he was raised. Doc looked past the way Kate chose to support herself. He understood the tragedies that could lead one to such a lowly state. They were alike in the sense that circumstance had forced them to abandon any respectability they might at one time have possessed. Kate and Doc had a strong connection, one she believed could never be challenged—that was until Wyatt Earp arrived at Fort Griffin in the fall of 1877. "I loved Doc," Kate admitted in her memoir. "I thought the world of him and liked his relations. He was always kind to me until he got mixed up with the Earps. That changed everything between Doc and me."[15]

According to Kate, when Wyatt Earp arrived in town "he had his wife Mattie with him." Born in Monmouth, Illinois, Earp had worked a variety of jobs before becoming a constable in Lamar, Missouri, in 1869. He was a former deputy town marshal at Dodge City when he rode into Fort Griffin. Celia Ann "Mattie" Blaylock, a one-time prostitute of note in various parts of Kansas, accompanied him. Wyatt was on the trail of a train robber and made his way to the Cattle Exchange Saloon to ask his friend John Shanssey if the criminal might have come through town. Shanssey didn't know but suggested Wyatt consult with his faro dealer. Doc and Wyatt were introduced, and, by the end of Wyatt's stay in Fort Griffin, a bond of friendship had been forged that would never be broken.[16]

Shanssey's Cattle Exchange Saloon, where Doc Holliday dealt cards in 1877
COURTESY OF LIBRARY OF CONGRESS

Kate was happy when Wyatt left Fort Griffin. She felt threatened by the amount of time Doc was spending with him. Historians speculate that Wyatt and Kate had met prior to his visit to Texas. His reference to her as Kate Fisher in his biography had led some to believe Wyatt made her acquaintance in Wichita when she was working for his sister-in-law. Kate makes no mention of a prior meeting with Wyatt in her memoir. She does recognize the influence Wyatt had on Doc and how it played on his desire for some respectability.[17]

Throughout the course of Doc's stay in Fort Griffin he had disagreements with losers at the faro table and cowboys who took offense to his dangerous wit and sharp tongue. Not that Doc ever asked, but Kate was always at the ready to intercede should it appear his life was in peril and those in disagreement with him had the upper hand.[18]

Wyatt Earp's recollection of such an occasion was recorded in the August 2, 1896, edition of the *San Francisco Examiner*. "It happened in 1877," the article began. "I had followed the trail of some cattle thieves across the border into Texas, and during a short stay in Fort Griffin I first met Doc Holliday and the woman who was known as Big Nose Kate, Kate Fisher and, on occasions of ceremony, Mrs. Doc Holliday. Holliday asked me a good many questions about Dodge City and seemed inclined to go there, but before he had made up his mind about it my business called me over to Fort Clark. It was while I was on my way back to Fort Griffin that my new friend and his Kate found it necessary to pull their stakes hurriedly. Where of the plain, unvarnished facts are these.

"Doc Holliday was spending the evening in a poker game, which was his custom whenever the faro bank did not present superior claims on his attention. On his right sat Ed Bailey, who needs no description because he is soon dropped from the narrative. The trouble began, as it was related to me afterward, by Ed Bailey monkeying with the deadwood, or what people who live in the cities call discards. Doc Holliday admonished him once or twice to 'play poker' which is your seasoned gambler's method of cautioning a friend to stop cheating, but the misguided Bailey persisted in his furtive attentions to the deadwood. Finally, having detected him again, Holliday pulled down a pot without showing his hand, which he had a perfect right to do. There upon Bailey started to throw his gun

Piedras Negras, a Mexican army post where Doc Holliday had a dental office
COURTESY OF LIBRARY OF CONGRESS

around on Holliday, as might have been expected. But before he could pull the trigger Doc Holliday had jerked a knife out of his breast pocket and with one sideways sweep had caught Bailey just below the brisket.

"Well, that broke up the game, and pretty soon Doc Holliday was sitting cheerfully in the front room of the hotel, guarded by the city marshal and a couple of policemen, while a hundred miners and gamblers clamored for his blood. You see, he had not lived in Fort Griffin very long, while Ed Bailey was well liked. It wasn't long before Big Nose Kate, who had a room downtown, heard about the trouble and went up to take a look at Doc through a back window. What she saw and heard led her to think that his life wasn't worth ten minutes' purchase, and I don't believe it was. There was a shed at the back of the lot, and a horse was stabled in it. She was a kind-hearted girl, was Kate, for she went to the trouble of leading the horses into the alley and tethering them there before she set fire to the shed. She also got a six-shooter from a friend down the street, which, with the one she always carried, made two.

"It happened just as she had planned it. The shed blazed up and she hammered at the door, yelling 'Fire!' Everybody rushed out, except the marshal, the constables and their prisoner. Kate walked in as bold as a lion, threw one of her six-shooters on the marshal and handed the other to Doc Holliday.

"'Come on, Doc,' she said with a laugh. He didn't need a second invitation, and the two of them backed out of the hotel, keeping the officers covered. All night they hid among the willows down by the creek, and early next morning a friend of Kate's brought them two horses and some of Doc's clothes from his room. Kate dressed up in a pair of pants, a pair of boots, a shirt and a hat, and the pair of them got away safely and rode four hundred miles to Dodge City."[19]

Wyatt Earp's account of Kate's daring rescue of Doc appeared in the book he cowrote with Stuart Lake. Kate insisted the tale was a lie. "Doc did not kill a man named Bailey in a fight over a poker game, nor was he arrested and locked up in a hotel room," she told writer Anton Mazzanovich. "Neither were natives cooking up a lynching bee. I certainly got a hearty laugh when I read that 'Big Nose Kate threw a few of her own and her lover's belongings into a bag, took two saddle ponies to a convenient spot, and then set fire to the rear end of the hotel. As the redoubtable woman had foreseen, every free man in Griffin but one ran out to fight the fire, and Doc was left with a single guard. Then Kate, with six-gun in hand, steps in the room and orders the surprised guard to throw up his hands, takes his guns and ammunition, rearms Doc with his favorite Colts, and hustles her lover out to the waiting ponies. And by the time the fire was put out and pursuit organized, Big Nose Kate and Doc were miles away on an unknown trail.'

"Just think of it . . . A woman weighing only one hundred sixteen pounds standing off a deputy, ordering him to throw up his hands, disarming him, rescuing her lover and hustling him to the waiting ponies. It reads fine, but there is not a word of truth in that fairy story."[20]

Kate recalls in her memoir that she and Doc left Fort Griffin in a rush bound for Dodge City. Although the dates Kate remembers these events to have occurred are questionable, there is no doubt of her movement with Doc Holliday at the time. They coincide with events written by historians such as Gary L. Roberts, author of *Doc Holliday: The Life and Legend*, and Karen Holliday Tanner.[21]

Kate and Doc made a few stops en route to Dodge. According to Kate, "We stopped at every place where there was money to be made at his profession [gambling]. We stayed awhile in Laredo then went to Eagle Pass. While there, Doc went across the Rio Grande to Piedras Negras, a Mexican army post, and called on the commanding officer to

Kate Elder and Doc Holliday spent a great deal of time in Eagle Pass, Texas.
CHRIS ENSS

inform him that he was a dentist. The commandant told Doc he would arrange quarters for him to practice in, and asked him to report next morning at 10 A.M."[22]

Eagle Pass, Texas, was established as a military post and was later known as an encampment for trappers, frontiersmen, and traders. Piedras Negras, where Doc worked, and the area around the army stockade was infested with outlaws. The area had grown into a location where cattle were driven, sold, and loaded onto trains bound for the East. Cattle thieves and fugitives of all kinds sought refuge at Eagle Pass and Piedras Negras.[23]

The town of Eagle Pass was face-to-face with Piedras Negras. The two spots were divided by the Rio Grande, which ran as if through a depression, between two rugged, uneven riverbanks covered in undergrowth. Small houses stood between the brambles and sometimes formed a street where cantinas and commerce abounded.[24]

Novelist and journalist Guillermo Prieto was in the area at roughly the same time Kate and Doc were there. "All signs of decorum, elegance, and even the memory of the cities of the United States seem to die at Eagle Pass," Prieto wrote about the spot in his memoir. "This is the bottom of the colander, the residue of the population, the sea shore on which foam and garbage are deposited."[25]

Both Kate and Doc thrived on the lawlessness of the two locations. The couple was continuously busy—Doc with his dental practice by day and dealing faro at night and Kate as a sporting woman with numerous clients. The burgeoning ranching industry caused their respective businesses to excel.[26]

Mexicans firing on soldiers and raiding parties threatening to invade the settlements eventually prompted Kate and Doc to pack their things and move on. "We remained in Eagle Pass for more than three months," Kate later recalled, "and Doc went across the river every morning. He made some money there, but when he left the commanding officer would not accept anything in the way of rent for the office Doc had occupied."[27]

Kate followed Doc to San Antonio "where he exchanged his Mexican pesos for American money," she noted in her memoir.[28] The Texas town served as the center of business for the border region and the Southwest. Cattlemen, merchants, and the military traveled to the area to buy livestock, sell a variety of goods from material to medicine, and man the army post. San Antonio was the last major city in the United States without train service. The railroad's arrival on February 16, 1877, further increased commerce in the city. Among the many enterprises in San Antonio were the unlawful trades. They, too, were experiencing a boom in business. The saloons were open continually as were many of the brothels.[29] Kate and Doc went right to work supplying the community with an honest faro game and company for the evening.

During Kate and Doc's time in San Antonio, the state of Texas was trying to bring about reform. The goal was to curtail gambling and eliminate prostitution. The January 10, 1879, edition of the *Marshall Messenger* noted that "many of the towns and cities in Texas are bankrupt in purse and rotten in morals" and that "change must be mandated."[30]

Mayors in places such as Dallas and Houston maintained that a "war against places of public prostitution as well as gambling halls must be waged." Officials in Galveston enacted ordinances to shut down all "bawdy

San Antonio, Texas, was another location Kate Elder and Doc Holliday frequented.
COURTESY OF UTSA SPECIAL COLLECTIONS

houses within a hundred-mile radius of the town." Police were dispatched nightly to the sporting homes, where the inmates were arrested. Political leaders were encouraging public servants in San Antonio to do the same. Kate's livelihood was being threatened.[31]

It's possible Kate knew of the directive issued by lawmakers in office in San Antonio in April 1878. The directive consisted of a dozen sections all designed to regulate disorderly houses and punish prostitutes. Section nine read, "Any courtesan, prostitute, bawdy or lewd woman or any female inmate of a bawdy house who shall be found wandering about the streets in the nighttime, or frequenting beer houses or places or public resort, shall be deemed guilty of a misdemeanor and be fined not less than five nor more than twenty-five dollars."[32]

Kate was no stranger to being arrested and was more than likely aware of the social stigma surrounding her profession. Being in business as long as she had been, she surely knew that local government benefited financially from those in her line of work and that politicians who knew the value of the funds generated by fast women would speak out in favor of the occupation. An article in the February 21, 1877, edition of the *Austin American-Statesman* advocated for a return to the system of licensing houses of ill fame rather than outright prohibition. "If an evil cannot be destroyed, root and branch, and if we find by the experience of this and all countries that it is least ruinous when regulated and controlled by law," the article read, "it becomes the providence of law makers to spurn Puritanical prejudices, and license and restrict curses which can only be ameliorated. Dram shops [saloons] may be exterminated because they who must drink will keep whiskey at home, and thus the evil is not popularized and everywhere operative. Here the flourishing gambling halls are frequented by old and young and yet the law fiercely interdicts the existence of these attractive half-hidden resorts of all classes."[33]

According to Kate, she stayed only a few weeks in San Antonio.[34] The political climate surrounding their work might have been the reason they moved on to a less populated town not far from another military post. Military garrisons attracted whiskey peddlers, gamblers, and prostitutes. The town of Brackettville, Texas, was close to Fort Clark. In fact, the two communities were across the river from one another. Fort Clark had a thousand people living there with six hundred of those being soldiers. The neighboring town of Brackettville was established in 1856. Stages en route to El Paso ran through the settlement. The troops stationed at Fort Clark generated a lively commerce in gambling and prostitution in Brackettville.[35] In the book *The Black Regulars, 1866–1898*, historians and authors William Dobak and Thomas Phillips noted that Brackettville was so wild and out of control with debauchery that the town should have been renamed Bordello.[36]

Kate and Doc's stay in the Texas town was brief; from Brackettville the pair traveled to Jacksboro, Texas.[37]

Fort Clark, Texas, where Doc Holliday, Kate Elder, and Wyatt Earp met in 1877
COURTESY OF LIBRARY OF CONGRESS

Jacksboro began as a small community of farmers and quickly grew in size and population to be named the county seat of Jack County. The troops from nearby Fort Richardson contributed to the rowdy nightlife as did the employers at the cotton gin and all the others who knew the town to be the number-one trading center along the Trinity River.[38]

Both Kate and Doc settled nicely into the riotous scene, taking up the same employment they had at the other undisciplined towns in the region. For a short while, the couple managed to do their jobs with little or no trouble, but their situation changed when a soldier challenged Doc's integrity. Bat Masterson wrote about the encounter in a book dedicated to the famous gunfighter.

Doc Holliday regarded himself as more than capable at handling card players who didn't like the way he dealt. Such was the case with the soldier who had been given permission by his commanding officer to visit Jacksboro. The soldier claimed he had been dealt a terrible hand and that

Doc had cheated him somehow. He tried to punctuate his feelings about the so-called crooked card game by going for his gun. Doc beat him to the draw and shot him dead. "This of course, necessitated the fighting Georgian taking another trip on the road," Bat wrote, "for he knew it would never do to let the soldiers at the fort capture him, which they would be sure to do as soon as word reached them about the killing of their comrade. He, therefore, lost no time in getting out of town and seated on the hurricane deck of a Texas cayuse, was well on his way to safety by the time the news of the homicide reached the fort." *[39]

Kate left Jacksboro with Doc. The pair rode hard over the open country toward the town Kate knew would be tolerant of their predicament, where saloons were endless and always open, gamblers had easy pickings, and sporting women were happily received—Dodge City.[40]

---

*Cayuse is an archaic term usually referring to a feral or low-quality horse or pony.

Chapter Four

Time in Dodge City

A HOT WIND USHERED KATE AND DOC INTO DODGE IN LATE MAY OF 1878. The sun's rays were like the flames of a furnace blasting down on the parched path leading into the city. The cow town had grown substantially in the short time Kate had been away. Dodge was never lacking in activity, but now it was a dizzying array of action. Hack drivers spurred their vehicles up and down the street at a rapid pace, unconcerned with the pedestrians who were forced to jump out of their way. Harlots stood outside the doorways of their closet-sized dens, inviting passersby to step inside. Stray dogs wandered about barking and scrounging for food. Ranch hands led bawling livestock into corrals or railroad cars. Disorderly drifters made their way to lively saloons, firing their pistols in the air as they went.[1]

The distant sound of voices, back-slapping laughter, profanity, and a piano's tinny repetitious melody wafted down Dodge City's thoroughfare. Kate and Doc were too tired to consider taking part in the liveliness and pressed on toward the Dodge House hotel which was adjacent to a billiard hall and restaurant. The well-known establishment would be their home for as long as they chose to stay in town.[2]

Dodge was just as Kate remembered it, only more so. It was an all-night town. Walkers and loungers kept the streets and saloons busy. Residents learned to sleep through the giggling, growling, and gunplay of the cowboy consumers and their paramours for hire. Kate and Doc were accustomed to the nightly frivolity and clatter. They were seldom disturbed by the commotion. Doc had no trouble falling asleep after the long, hard ride. Kate, on the other hand, decided to take a position on the

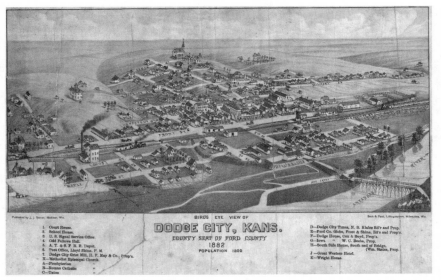

Bird's-eye view of Dodge City, Kansas COURTESY OF KANSAS STATE HISTORICAL SOCIETY

balcony of the hotel to make sure no one with any ill feelings toward Doc had followed the pair from Texas. She would rest only after it seemed Doc was safe.[3]

According to Kate, she and Doc were registered at the Dodge House as Mr. and Mrs. Holliday.[4] Doc set up a dental practice in the large room the pair occupied at the hotel. There were three doctors living in Dodge City at the time; none were dentists, although in an emergency they had removed a bothersome tooth or two. Doc received many referrals from the physicians in town, and his patient list had grown. To help the practice along, he placed an ad in the June 27, 1878, edition of the *Dodge City Times*.[5]

"Dentistry. J. H. Holliday, Dentist, very respectfully offers his professional services to the citizens of Dodge City and surrounding country during the summer. Office at Room No. 24, Dodge House. Where satisfaction is not given money will be refunded."[6]

Kate continued working in her chosen profession. There were several places in Dodge where sporting women could be found. The most popular locations were the Long Branch Saloon, the Crystal Palace, the Saratoga, the Varieties, and Beatty and Kelley's. Many of the best-known saloons in town had rooms in the back where soiled doves conducted business. In mid-1878 that business was kept as much of a secret as could be because a city ordinance against prostitution was in effect. The ordinance was not issued in the hopes of bringing about reform. The cost to retain quality law enforcement agents had ballooned, and city leaders believed the fines made from citing prostitutes would cover the salaries.[7] "These fines are extended to the houses of ill fame and those who inhabit them," an article in the August 10, 1878, edition of the *Dodge City Times* explained. "The

Dodge City, Kansas COURTESY OF KANSAS STATE HISTORICAL SOCIETY

frail humanity will respond to the demand of the depleted city exchequer, remember that the wages of sin is death. The 'girls' will feel that they are not answering the Great Tribunal, though their temporary care is under the brawny arms of a big policeman, who is sworn to protect the peace and dignity of the city.

"City scrip had fallen fifty centers on the dollar, but upon the announcement of the passage of the ordinance herein mentioned, suddenly rose, and now commands eighty-five cents on the dollar, a higher market rate than previously. Under this prudent dispensation we shall soon see the city debt liquidation and scrip at practically zero.

"To feel the potency of either moral or statute laws is to feel the reign of security, comfort and happiness. Every human being pays tribute. The sporting man or the frail sister of humanity will recognize while there is just retribution there is a just demand for the protection of themselves as well as for those who are at peace with God and their fellow man."[8]

The Dodge City ordinance regarding the arrest and fining of prostitutes was strictly enforced. Kate managed to avoid any encounters with the law, but some of her competitors didn't fare as well. Between June and August 1878 more than $200 in fines were collected. Several fast women decided to leave town after they were detained. "The community is well without them," an article in the August 17, 1878, edition of the Dodge City Times proclaimed. "The operation of the ordinance proved as we expected—the ridding of a class of deadbeats, thieves and eyesores."[9]

There were those who believed that suppressing such crimes was futile. "Gambling and prostitution are paragons compared to that system of highway robbery that the law seems powerless to reach," some citizens complained. "It is not necessary to recount the impediments in the way of lawful protection, but we are aware that there is eventually a summary tribunal that does not deal gently with thieves and robbers."[10]

As a frequent visitor to Dodge City's many public houses, Kate was witness to the types of criminal behavior citizens thought more important to eliminate than prostitution. She was present at the Long Branch Saloon the evening Assistant U. S. Deputy Marshal Harry T. McCarty was shot and killed. The assistant marshal was having a drink at the bar

Front Street in Dodge City, Kansas COURTESY OF KANSAS STATE HISTORICAL SOCIETY

when a drunken cowboy staggered over to him, grabbed the lawman's gun out of his holster, and fired. A bystander shot the drunk, but McCarty bled to death.[11]

Kate was also present when Marshal Wyatt Earp and policeman Jim Masterson were called in to take care of a quartet of sheepherders firing their guns into businesses along Front Street and into the Lady Gay Saloon where Doc Holliday was dealing cards. Earp and Masterson arrived on the scene with the intention of arresting the men and taking away their firearms. Shots were exchanged between the rowdies and the lawmen, and George Hoyt, one of the herders, was hit. The wounded man was taken to the doctor, but the injury proved to be too serious to treat. Hoyt died a few days after the incident.[12]

The Comique Theater was another favorite spot Kate liked to visit and meet potential clients. The theater was located inside the Lady Gay Saloon and played host to such popular entertainers as comedian Eddie Foy and musician Jimmie Thompson. Kate was present at the playhouse on August 17, 1878, when an inebriated gunman opened fire on the stage acts. Fortunately, no one was injured. Kate's line of work naturally meant she would be exposed to dangerous situations. It was a part of the profession she would gladly have done without. Kate belonged to a segment of the frontier's female workforce that significantly rebelled against the oppressive gender role that Americans of the staid Victorian era sought to impose upon women of the day. The cost for such rebellion was the occasional gunfight.[13]

According to Kate, she and Doc rarely had major arguments. They enjoyed one another's company and would often socialize with members of the Dodge City sporting crowd. The crowd consisted of lawman turned gunfighter Joshua Webb, lawman and gambler Bat Masterson, and saloon owners Luke Short, William H. Harris, and Chalk Beeson. All the men were congenial, and their paramours and wives were equally hospitable. Wyatt Earp and Mattie Blaylock joined the group at times for meals or to see a show at the Comique. Doc, Kate, Wyatt, and Mattie had met in Texas, but they had no real opportunity for a friendship to form. The same could be said for the limited contact the four had in Dodge City from May to July of 1878. In August an event occurred that changed the nature of their association and, in Kate's estimation, forever altered her relationship with the man she regarded as her "everything."[14]

On August 18, 1878, a group of cowboys from the Kenedy Ranch in Texas poured into the Comique Theater and overtook the bar area. Most of the men were already drunk, and they proceeded to get even more so. They were loud and obnoxious and looking for a fight. The leader of the unruly ranch hands was James Kenedy. He was a tall man with a strong build, and he was accustomed to getting his own way. He wore tailor-made clothes and carried himself with confidence derived mostly from his family's sizeable bank account and landholdings.[15]

The bartender objected to Kenedy and his friends pushing all the customers out of the way and for venturing behind the bar and helping themselves to drinks. He ordered them out from behind the bar and requested they settle themselves down. James took offense to the bartender's tone, and an argument ensued. Wyatt Earp was called in to diffuse the situation. His presence only caused the trouble to escalate.[16]

The altercation became physical with cowhands rushing the lawmen and Earp fighting them off by bashing them in the skull with the butt of his six-shooter. The activity filtered out the saloon and into the street in front of the establishment. Earp was surrounded by cowboys. According to the August 20, 1878, edition of the *Globe-Republican*, "Several shots were accidentally fired which created general confusion among the crowd of persons present."[17]

Doc was playing cards and could see the incident unfolding from the table where he was dealing. He noticed that Earp was alone in the fight and that any backup might arrive too late. Doc turned to fellow gambler Frank Loving seated next to him and asked him if he had a six-shooter. Loving handed his gun to Doc. The armed dentist removed his own gun from his holster and walked into the street carrying two six-shooters. "Throw up your hands," he announced. The cowboys that were pressing in on Earp looked up at Doc. In an instant the lawman drew his weapon, and the arrest of the crowd followed. Earp led them to the jail for an overnight stay. They were fined and released the following day.[18]

"We are glad to chronicle the fact that none were seriously hurt, and nobody shot," the *Globe-Republican* article noted. "We however cannot help but regret the too ready use of pistols in all rows of such character and would like to see a greater spirit of harmony exist between our officers and cattlemen so that snarling cayotes [sic] and killers could make their own fights without interesting or dragging good men into them."[19]

Doc Holliday's willingness to help Wyatt Earp in his time of need forged a bond between the two that would never be broken. Kate noticed a significant change in her relationship with Doc after the incident. "He was always kind," Kate would repeat again and again in her memoir, "until

Long Branch Saloon in Dodge City COURTESY OF KANSAS STATE HISTORICAL SOCIETY

he got mixed up with the Earps." Kate would have to compete for Doc's affections whenever Wyatt was around.[20]

Over the years, Kate and Wyatt would come to despise one another. Kate saw Wyatt as someone who interfered in her life with Doc. Unlike Wyatt, Doc accepted Kate for what she was and never tried to reform her. Kate treated Doc the same. Tempers flared, and heated words were exchanged at times when the pair had too much to drink. Wyatt made mention of such behavior in Stuart Lake's book of the lawman. "Their relationship had its temperamental ups and downs," Wyatt is quoted as saying in *Wyatt Earp: Frontier Marshal*. "And when Kate was writhing under Doc's scorn she'd get drunk as well as furious and make Doc more trouble than a shooting spree." On more than one occasion, Wyatt suggested that Doc should "belt her one." Doc would reply, "A man cannot do what he wants to in this world, but only that which will benefit him."[21]

It was no secret to Kate that Doc had once been madly in love with his first cousin Mattie. Mattie was refined, petite, and soft spoken. She was everything Kate wasn't. Doc would often fall into a depression over his lost love and lash out publicly at Kate for not being the lady he could have had.[22]

One night in September 1878, just after such a show, Doc returned to the Dodge House to sleep off another night of drinking and forget the spectacle he had made of himself and Kate. A furious Kate followed him to the hotel, banging loudly on the locked door. Doc was having a coughing fit and couldn't make it up off the bed to let her in. Kate burst down the door and bounded into the room with a pistol in her hand. "You lousy son-of-a-bitch!" she yelled. "I'm going to fill you full of so many holes you won't float in brine!" Kate fired a shot into the mattress Doc was lying on. He jumped up, jerked the gun out of her hand, and cracked her over the head with it. Kate fell to the floor bleeding. Doc stood over her, feeling sober and sorry. The two were not seen again until late the following afternoon when they were holding hands and behaving like newlyweds.[23]

Kate was jealous of the time Doc spent with the Earps, specifically Wyatt. It was not uncommon for her to question Doc about what he would be doing with them and where they would be going. Wyatt overheard an exchange between the two about Doc's plans, and Wyatt began referring to her as Big-Nose Kate. It was a nickname Kate was greatly offended by and one that would stick with her always.[24]

As fall turned to winter and the Kansas weather became increasingly cold, Doc's health began to decline. Most consumption or tuberculosis

Varieties Dance Hall, Dodge City COURTESY OF KANSAS STATE HISTORICAL SOCIETY

patients sought a cure for the disease in sanitariums. It was believed by experts in the field of study that rest and healthful climate could change the course of the illness. It was also thought to be somewhat treatable through good hygiene. Tuberculosis patients with mustaches or beards were deemed in the most danger because facial hair was thought to be a breeding ground for the disease. Doc was not willing to rest nor shave off his mustache. He had tried to seek out healthy climates. Dodge City in the summer was fine when the hacking, bloody coughs, debilitating pain in his lungs, and fatigue were at a minimum. Cold weather was hazardous for Doc. It was difficult to breathe in frigid air. Whenever Doc was exposed to such temperatures and couldn't get around, Kate would sit beside him during coughing attacks and try to ease his pain. She would insist he rest and stay with him as he slept.[25]

In May 1878 it was estimated that one-fifth of mankind would die of consumption within the year. Kate was determined that Doc wouldn't be among them. The couple discussed moving to Colorado. The skies were sunnier and the climate drier. A series of gold and silver rushes had made the region an attractive destination for fortune hunters. Kate and Doc could easily find work among the prospectors hoping to discover the mother lode.[26]

The decision when to leave Kansas had not been made. Until the exact time came around, Kate stayed busy entertaining cowhands in Dodge City and soldiers from Fort Dodge. When Doc was feeling well, he was taking care of his dental practice and playing cards with individuals of questionable character. A pair of robberies in a short time should have led law enforcement to suspect the shady gamblers in Doc's association. Instead, the law was led to suspect Doc had a part in the crimes.[27]

On December 11, 1878, an attempt was made to burglarize the Blue Front Store owned by Jacob Collar. The robber entered the business from the rear and proceeded to the money drawers in front. The drawers were filled with cash. In whittling away at the wood to gain entrance to the drawers, the burglar struck the alarm bell which awakened Jacob. The December 14, 1878, edition of the *Dodge City Times* reported that Jacob "drove off the nocturnal scamps before they secured the booty." This was the first attempted robbery of the kind that ever occurred in Dodge. A

John Henry (Doc) Holliday COURTESY OF KANSAS STATE HISTORICAL SOCIETY

witness claimed to have seen the culprit and claimed that the activities of "an ailing gambler" would be watched closely from now on. There was only one "ailing gambler" in Dodge City, and Kate could vouch for Doc Holliday's whereabouts on the night of the attempted crime.[28]

Days later Doc was implicated in another robbery, this one involving missing money from Wright and Beverly's Store. The mercantile in question was owned by one of Dodge City's most respected citizens, Robert M. Wright. Charles Wright, a relative of Robert's, had access to the business and was the most likely suspect. He was a dishonest gambler with a dubious reputation. Charles ran a series of crooked card games designed specifically to swindle players out of their money. Charles and Doc knew one another, and when the funds went missing from the store, he accused Doc of taking it. Robert believed Charles when he told him he had nothing to do with the theft and applauded his family member for having the strength to call out the man who had.[29] It didn't make any difference how much Kate insisted Doc couldn't have been involved; she was a fallen woman, and, in many circles, fallen women were all thought to be liars.[30]

The combination of being wrongfully accused and Doc's health issues prompted Kate and Doc to move along. If they'd stayed in Dodge they'd be drawn into a lawsuit they could neither afford nor possessed the right reputation to fight. Leaving Kansas was the best option. Kate and Doc rode out of town bound for New Mexico. Doc had heard that New Mexico was a good environment for those suffering with tuberculosis. The strain of the trip proved to be too much for Doc, however. The disease had overtaken him from inside out. Fluid filled his lungs, and he hacked and spit constantly.[31]

The couple made several stops on the journey. At one point, Kate had to help Doc off his horse to a comfortable spot on the ground near a tree. Doc would cough uncontrollably, bringing up bile and bloodstained fluid. Kate would clean off his face and dispose of the soiled handkerchiefs and towels containing the phlegm and other substances. Neither thought anything of her handling the sullied rags. Tuberculosis was then believed to be hereditary and not contagious.[32]

The distance between Dodge City and Las Vegas, New Mexico, was more than 350 miles. Kate suspected Doc was too ill to go that far, so the

Kate Elder COURTESY OF THE SHARLOT HALL MUSEUM AND LIBRARY AND ARCHIVES, C-230
ITEM 3, FOLDER 1, BOX 7

pair decided to travel to Trinidad, Colorado, instead. The mining town was close, and Doc could rest a while before continuing to New Mexico.[33]

Trinidad was on the Santa Fe Trail and was a bustling spot filled with coal miners working the valuable find discovered in 1862. The Atchison, Topeka, and Santa Fe Railroad had made its way to the area a few months prior to Kate and Doc's arrival. As a result, the town was quickly becoming a nerve center for ranching operations.[34] If Doc had been feeling better, he probably would have found a table at one of the many local saloons. Kate most certainly would have returned to her trade as well, but Doc was sick and needed complete bed rest. Physicians who had examined Doc in Dodge City had prescribed "rest in bed or in an armchair for at least six months in order to give the body a chance to gain strength to fight the disease." Doc would never allow himself to be down that long. He would stay put long enough to recover and return to his usual activities.[35]

Kate Elder and Doc Holliday took refuge in Trinidad, Colorado, en route to New Mexico. THE DENVER PUBLIC LIBRARY, WESTERN HISTORY COLLECTION, X-1936

To live comfortably in a climate conducive to healing, tuberculosis sufferers had to either possess or earn a substantial amount of money. Doc and Kate had been able to save a few dollars for whatever might come, but neither had any idea if it would be enough. Both had a taste for opulent living—fine food, cigars, and hotels. The need for more spurred Doc to get back on his feet as soon as he could.[36]

Kate maintains that Doc remained in bed during the entire time they were in Trinidad, but Bat Masterson wrote that Doc got a game going one evening at the town's best gambling hall. A young gambler named Kid Colton sat down at the ailing dentist's table and proceeded to lose. Frustrated with the cards he'd been dealt and hungry to make a name for himself by challenging Doc, Kid Colton goaded him into a gunfight. The pair met on the street, and before Kid Colton's six-shooter cleared his holster, Doc had fired his weapon twice, hitting the overly confident high roller in the chest and killing him instantly. There are no newspaper accounts or police records to corroborate Doc's encounter with Kid Colton. Kate makes no mention of it in any of her writings either.[37]

After ten days, Doc was well enough to travel, but it was doubtful he could make it to New Mexico without another attack. Kate made arrangements with the head driver of a freight wagon company to escort them to Las Vegas. Doc would make the journey south lying in the back of a prairie schooner. Kate never left his side.[38]

Chapter Five

Leaving Las Vegas

The main street of Las Vegas, New Mexico, was so crowded the passing streams of people moved as if unseen hands were dragging them this way and that. In addition to the throngs of people crossing back and forth across the dusty thoroughfare, there were teams of horses pulling buckboards and business buggies, cowhands leading their mounts to the livery, and ranchers hauling supplies in and out of town. Kate and Doc added to the chaos when they arrived just before Christmas 1878. After tending to their rides and securing a room at the Adobe Hotel in Gallinas Canyon, north of the central plaza of town, Kate put Doc to bed. He was coughing a wet cough that produced enough blood to saturate a handkerchief. Doc wasn't the only tuberculosis sufferer in Las Vegas. Many patients had gathered in the New Mexico location. Dry air and rest were the only remedies for the disease. Sometimes bundled in blankets and sheltered from precipitation, patients there endured outdoor life in all weather, hoping the regimen would heal their damaged lungs.[1]

Tuberculosis patients also sought to rid themselves of the disease by soaking in the hot springs six miles northwest of town. The September 30, 1878, edition of the *Daily Gazette* noted that the hot springs near Las Vegas contained the same mineral constituents as those in Hot Springs, Arkansas, and Thermal Springs in Europe. Frontier physicians recommended soaking in the calcium- and sodium-enriched hot springs because the bicarbonates boosted blood circulation, reduced pain, and repaired tissue damage.[2] According to Kate, she tried to convince Doc to consider staying put until his health was somewhat restored. She hoped he would take advantage of the hot springs and the rest. The attack he had in Dodge City had left him weak and unsteady on his feet. Kate promised to provide for them both while he was recovering, but Doc refused to go along with her plan.[3]

As soon as Doc was able, he located office space on Bridge Street and opened his practice. Las Vegas was a stopping-off point for those traveling along the Santa Fe Trail; it was the biggest city between San Francisco and Independence, Missouri. Doc anticipated there would be many people in need of a dentist. The army post, Fort Union, was twenty miles north of Las Vegas, and soldiers routinely spent time in town enjoying the nightlife. If Doc's practice faltered for any reason, he could also sustain himself at the poker table. Las Vegas continually played host to cavalrymen, desperados, and outlaws looking for a fast game. The number of card players eager to be separated from their money swelled when the Atchison, Topeka, and Santa Fe Railroad reached the area. Before Doc had an opportunity to fully fleece amateur card sharps, the New Mexico territorial legislature passed a bill prohibiting gambling. The law didn't stop Doc from dealing, however; he kept his games of chance quiet while maintaining the semblance of an upstanding citizen as the community's respectable dentist.[4]

Las Vegas wasn't as well-known as other Wild West towns like Deadwood, South Dakota, or Dodge City, Kansas, but it had a reputation for being the worst of the worst in the West. In 1882 Ralph Emerson Twitchell, mayor of nearby Santa Fe, noted that Las Vegas was a "most disagreeable destination." He went on to add, "Without exception there is no town which harbors a more disreputable gang of desperados and outlaws than Las Vegas."[5]

Kate flourished in disagreeable locations. Many soiled doves did. Kate would do well for herself in Las Vegas. It was a thriving trade center with more than two thousand inhabitants, with large stores, a few hotels, saloons, and gambling halls. Kate danced at the various saloons and gambling halls in town in the early evening then entertained specific patrons once the stage show was over. According to Kate, she would travel an hour away from Las Vegas to Santa Fe, New Mexico, for the same reason. Two of her favorite stops there were the Broad-Gauge Saloon and Billiard Hall and the Beer Hall and Depot Saloon. Both businesses

Las Vegas, New Mexico CHRIS ENSS

were situated in the public square in the heart of the city. There was never a shortage of men who wanted to spend time with the woman who by day called herself Mrs. John Henry Holliday. Kate's favors were in high demand, and as a result, she earned more than $200 a week. Her income increased with a percentage from the "dollar a bottle" beer the establishments sold as well as from the "five dollar a quart" wine that was offered.[6]

Kate not only spent time with cowboys and miners in the New Mexico establishments but with prominent businessmen and civil leaders as well. In March 1879 a special committee of the board of health in Las Vegas met to discuss an ordinance that would require all sporting women to purchase a license. An article in the March 23, 1879, edition of the *Las Vegas Gazette* noted that "strong pressure would be brought to bear in the council against the adoption of such an ordinance." According to Kate, the push for licensing was introduced by the wives of some of the men who had kept company with her. They wanted a portion of the fees collected for licensing soiled doves and houses of ill repute to be siphoned into a fund to help build a new school.[7]

An ordinance requiring that prostitutes purchase a license to conduct business might not have been approved, but it did not stop the respectable women in Santa Fe and Las Vegas from submitting letters about the issue. A letter in the April 14, 1879, edition of the *Las Vegas Gazette* highlighted the frustration some women had with the sporting girls. "I have knowledge of how over a several month period a smitten youth spent $20,000 on one of the most popular street nymphs in the city," one woman wrote. "$20,000! You wouldn't catch them spending $20,000 on a decent woman. Oh, those men!"[8]

When Kate and Doc weren't working they spent time with friends, fellow gamblers, and business owners—one of whom was a jeweler named William Leonard. Leonard and Doc operated out of the same building. He, too, suffered with tuberculosis. Like Doc, Leonard's background wasn't pristine. He'd had a few run-ins with the law and was not a stranger to settling disputes with a gun. Three months prior to Kate and Doc's arrival in Las Vegas, Leonard had shot a police officer named Jose Mares as he stood outside a mercantile in the city plaza. Leonard was arrested on the charge of intent to kill and released on bail pending a hearing. Friends of the wounded officer then attacked Leonard for what he had done. Six months after the violent incident, a local grand jury handed down an indictment against Leonard. In March 1879 Leonard decided to leave town before his hearing. Kate, Doc, and Leonard wouldn't see one another again until the couple traveled to Tombstone.[9]

In addition to losing a good friend to the pressures of Las Vegas laws, Kate and Doc's livelihood was threatened by the same institutions. Civic leaders in Las Vegas and Santa Fe were speaking out against such vices as prostitution and gambling. An article in the January 11, 1879, edition of the *Weekly New Mexican* noted that "the man who has squandered his patrimony in drinking, gambling, and loose women has no claim an honest community is bound to respect." Respectable citizens who believed gambling was an act of risking something of value on the outcome of a game that may be determined in part or entirely by chance urged lawmakers to do something about the proliferation of gambling in the region. In

Kate Elder and Doc Holliday arrived in Las Vegas just before Christmas in 1878.

January 1879 a bill prohibiting gambling in the New Mexico Territory was passed.[10]

Doc Holliday, operating out of a saloon and gambling hall on Center Street at this time, didn't let the ordinance stop him from doing business. His flagrant disregard for the law ultimately posed trouble for him in March 1879 when he was indicted for "keeping [a] gaming table called Monte." Doc pled guilty to the charge and was fined $25, plus court costs of $1.75.[11]

The arrival of the Atchison, Topeka, and Santa Fe Railroad into Las Vegas changed the financial landscape of the town. Doc decided to take advantage of the increase in visitors that would be arriving by building his own saloon. In late July he and his partner, Jordan Webb, leased a parcel of land a block away from the railroad station to have their establishment constructed. The Holliday Saloon was a one-story affair with overlapping, wooden siding. Kate would be welcome in the business, but county deeds and records make it clear she had no vested interest in the property.[12]

Within the first month of operation, the law called on the owners of the Holliday Saloon twice. Both times Doc was fined for illegal activity. In mid-August he was indicted for "keeping [a] gaming table and for carrying a deadly weapon." Owing to the gambling moratorium and the slow dental trade, Doc left Las Vegas on a stage bound for Otero, New Mexico. From there he caught the train for Dodge City, Kansas. Kate remained behind to help manage Doc's affairs at the saloon and continue with her own line of business.[13]

The lovers were reunited in late summer of 1879. Doc had returned with a substantial amount of money, all of which he acquired for helping Deputy Marshal Bat Masterson handle a job for the Santa Fe Railroad. Not everyone was pleased to see Doc back in New Mexico walking arm in arm with Kate, now a well-known sporting woman in the territory.[14]

Many residents in Santa Fe and Las Vegas disagreed with the kind of life Kate and Doc led. An article in the July 20, 1881, edition of the *Las Vegas Optic* included comments about the low nature most believed the couple possessed. "Doc was always considered a shiftless, bagged-legged character—a killer and professional cut-throat and not a wit [sic] too refined to rob stages or even steal sheep. The woman, Elder, was a

Kate did business in Santa Fe, New Mexico, as well as Las Vegas.
COURTESY PALACE OF THE GOVERNORS PHOTO ARCHIVES, #131753

Santa Fe tid-bit and surrounded her habiliment with [a] detestable odor before leaving [the] ancient city that will, in itself, make her memory immortal.'"[15]

Kate and Doc were never ones to let public opinion change their behavior. According to Kate, the pair was quite content in New Mexico

* Habiliment is another word for clothing.

69

Kate and Doc's business flourished when the Atchison, Topeka, and Santa Fe Railroad reached Las Vegas. COURTESY PALACE OF THE GOVERNORS PHOTO ARCHIVES, #015870

and had no intentions of leaving no matter what anyone else thought. Although Doc's dental practice had been lacking in patients since they arrived, the two enjoyed their time together out and about town in the evenings. Kate boasted that while in Las Vegas, "Doc's reputation was good and that his conduct was always that of a gentleman."[16]

On July 26, 1879, Doc's conduct was anything but gentlemanly. He was suspected of shooting a drunken hell-raiser by the name of Mike Gordon. The July 29, 1879, edition of the *Las Vegas Gazette* reported that Gordon had been drinking heavily and threatening to shoot out all the lights in a new dance hall on Railroad Avenue. He tried to persuade his girlfriend, who was working at a similar establishment on Center Street, to accompany him on his shooting spree, but she refused. Gordon was furious and promised to either kill someone or be killed by morning.[17]

The killing of Mike Gordon occurred a few moments later outside the Center Street dance hall. The newspaper article noted that the man was belligerent and firing his weapon into the dance hall where his girl-friend was employed.[18]

"Gordon was standing to the right of the hall after some of his threats and drew a revolver and fired, the bullet passing through the pants legs of a Mexican and struck in the floor next to the bartender who was standing at the rear of the bar," the *Las Vegas Gazette* report read. "Other shots were fired immediately, but it is difficult to tell how or who by.

"It is said that Gordon fired a second shot. Every person there says three shots were fired, while several maintain that five in all were fired. Gordon at once ceased firing and disappeared. An hour or two later, a Mr. Kennedy went into his tent, some thirty or forty yards away, to go to bed and hearing groans investigated and found Gordon lying on the ground outside. The news soon spread, and his woman arriving at the scene had him taken to her room east of the court house where he died at 6 o'clock Sunday morning. In the afternoon, the coroner held an inquest, and the jury returned a verdict of excusable homicide."[19]

Doc had problems with Gordon at his saloon that evening, and it wasn't too difficult to believe he would have shot him. He never owned up to killing him, and no charges were brought against him. Gordon died from a gunshot wound to the chest. If there were any witnesses, no one came forward—most felt a public service had been done. Friends insisted someone did see Doc shoot Gordon, but fear of the volatile dentist kept them from admitting what they knew.[20]

In his book *Famous Gunfighters of the Western Frontier*, Bat Masterson revealed that Doc Holliday was responsible for Gordon's death. According to him, the two men quarreled inside the Center Street saloon where Doc was working, and Doc invited Gordon to meet him outside in the street. Gordon obliged, and, as soon as he "stepped from the door, Doc shot him dead."[21]

According to Kate, in building the saloon it seemed Doc had established roots. She allowed herself to believe they were now settled and would live their lives together forever in New Mexico. It might have been if not for the arrival of Wyatt Earp, his brothers, and their wives.[22]

On Saturday, October 18, 1879, Doc "ran across" Wyatt Earp, Mattie Blaylock, Wyatt's brother Jim and his wife, Bessie, and their daughter, Hattie, at the "Plaza in Old Town." According to Kate, the party was on their way to Arizona. Wyatt shared news of a silver strike in southern

William Barclay "Bat" Masterson

Bat Masterson CHRIS ENSS

Arizona and invited Doc to visit their camp outside town so he could tell him more about the exciting prospects that lay ahead.[23]

Kate was opposed to Doc spending time with Wyatt and cited as her reason that she believed the team of horses the Earps were traveling with were stolen. Wyatt must have overheard Kate's objections because it was at this time he began to refer to her as Big-Nose Kate. Wyatt Earp biographer Casey Tefertiller indicates that Wyatt gave her the name because "she nosed into areas that were none of her business."[24]

Kate resented the Earps' intrusion into the life she was enjoying with Doc in Las Vegas and fought to hold on to it. She tried to convince Doc to keep his distance from Wyatt. She reminded him of all they had in New Mexico and how business was sure to increase at the Holliday Saloon now that the railroad line had made it to Las Vegas. Doc refused to listen. "The stormy part of Doc's life commenced when he decided to join Wyatt Earp," Kate wrote. "We pulled out [of Las Vegas] the next afternoon. There were seven of us in that outfit."[25]

The trip from Las Vegas west toward northern Arizona to Prescott took close to a month. According to Kate, she and Doc "traveled in the same wagon as Wyatt and Mattie." The farther Kate got from New Mexico, the more her resentment toward the Earps, and Wyatt in particular, grew. Not only had they disrupted her life with Doc, but she also had to compete for his attention whenever Wyatt was around. Kate didn't trust Wyatt either. She believed he was less than honest and cited a specific incident on the trail she felt proved her suspicions. "At one time [during the trip to Arizona] we camped several days," Kate later wrote. "Wyatt opened his trunk before his wife, Doc, and me and showed us false mustaches, beards and wigs and he asked me if I knew what they were. I said 'Yes, I think I do.'"[26]

Kate, Doc, and the Earps arrived in Prescott in November 1879. According to Kate, Wyatt and the others went to stay with his brother Virgil who was living in town. Virgil and his wife, Allie, had arrived in Prescott in 1878. Kate and Doc camped in the wagon before checking into a hotel the following day.[27]

Gold had been discovered in the Prescott area in 1863 and the community quickly erupted with hopeful prospectors seeking their fortunes.

Kate and Doc traveled to Prescott, Arizona, in late 1879. CHRIS ENSS

The thriving town then became the capital of Arizona. Doc had no trouble finding a fast faro game at one of the saloons in the mining hamlet.[28]

Kate and Doc's relationship was strained by early December 1879. The Earps were eager to depart the area for Tombstone, where numerous silver-rich claims were being filed. They wanted to get there before the silver played out, and they wanted Doc to go with them. Kate once again expressed her desire that Doc stay with her. "It was there that Doc and I had the first disagreement, or misunderstanding, since we had been married," Kate recalled in her memoir. "It came about because I wanted him to remain in Prescott. When Wyatt and Jim started for Tombstone, Doc did not go with them but promised to join them in Tombstone later on."[29]

Doc's decision to remain in Prescott might have had more to do with the success he was having at the gambling tables than with his devotion to Kate. He continued to reap the rewards, dealing faro until March 1880. City leaders enacted a series of ordinances pertaining to gambling, and the fines levied against all who refused to comply were substantial. In addition to the monthly evaluation of gaming tables that were taking place, gamblers were required to purchase a license to operate a game. The cost of the license was $500 a quarter.[30]

Kate anticipated the new gambling regulations would make Doc want to leave Prescott. Daily, she made a case for him to stay and held out hope that her being in town would be enough to make him want to remain in central Arizona. A letter from Wyatt urging Doc to come to Tombstone was all the itinerant gambler and dentist needed to persuade him to move on. Kate was crushed and angry. "If you're going to tie yourself to the Earp brothers, go to it. I'm going to Globe," she remembered telling him. Kate didn't want to stay in Prescott without Doc. She didn't want to be without him at all but recognized the hold the Earps had on him. "All right, I will be in Globe in a few days, too," Doc told Kate. "I don't think I will like it in Tombstone anyway."[31]

According to Kate, she and Doc left Prescott together and stayed overnight at a mining town while en route. "We had a time finding accommodations. There was no rooming house or anything like it there. At last we went to the superintendent [of the mine], a Mr. Webber. He gave us a bed in his office. It was a good bed, too. There was a store there, and we had a kind of breakfast [the] next morning. We started out again." Doc continued to Tombstone, and Kate traveled to Globe.[32]

Globe was a busy and sometimes violent location. It was not unlike many of the places Kate had lived and worked. She "owned and operated a miner's boarding house called The Globe," where several wild characters spent time. In a letter to her niece Lillian Rafferty in 1940, Kate claimed to have made a $500 deposit on the property. According to Kate, she missed Doc and continuously wished she'd been able to "get him away from the Earps." Evidently, Doc was missing Kate too. "I used to get letters from Doc to come to Tombstone, begging to pay him a visit," Kate later recalled. Once her business was established, she did make the journey to see the man she continued to refer to as her husband.[33]

In a year's time, she made three trips to southern Arizona to see Doc. The time he'd spent in Tombstone had changed him. He had become cold and distant. "I was never afraid of Doc," Kate mentioned in her memoir. "I found him with another woman in Tombstone. I had a big knife with me at the time, and I said that I'd rip her open. He came away from her because I wasn't afraid of him." Kate blamed the company he kept for his detached, almost hostile, attitude toward her. According to Kate, Wyatt Earp was responsible for what had transpired, and she would hold him responsible for what was yet to come.[34]

CHAPTER SIX

Street Fight in Tombstone

IT WAS A CHILLY EVENING IN MID-MARCH 1881. KATE HAD TRAVELED from Globe to Tombstone to see Doc. According to her, she had made the trip at his request. She noted in her memoir that they lost no time settling their differences. The smoke from an oil lamp in his room coiled wraithlike to the ceiling, smirching the cobwebs that festooned the top of the faded curtains. Kate studied the sad-looking window coverings in the reflection of the mirror into which she was staring. She had been pinning her hair up and playing with a pair of earrings when she noticed the breeze from the partially opened window ruffle the curtains. Kate anticipated spending a great deal of time with Doc in the room and pondered whether to update the décor.[1]

Doc had taken up residence on Sixth Street in a small boarding house positioned between a funeral parlor and a winery. The furnishing was sparse and covered with dust. Kate's things were scattered about the room. Doc had promised to take her to dinner when he returned from the errand he had rushed off to handle. Once she finished getting ready for the night out, she turned her attention to a copy of the *Arizona Weekly Citizen* lying on a chair by the door. A story about a murder and an attempted stage robbery twenty-eight miles from Tombstone caught her eye.[2]

"Detective R. H. Paul was on the box with the driver at the time, and his double-barreled Winchester rested by his side," the March 20, 1881, article noted. "It is believed that the Cow-boys were completely surprised to find Paul upon the stage, as no two of them would attempt to tackle Paul. At the first word, 'Hold!' Paul coolly reached for his gun, exclaiming, 'By God! I hold for nobody!' It is a question who fired first, Paul or the robbers; but the crack of the rifles were almost simultaneous, frightening the leaders into a run. Paul emptied both barrels of his gun, and his revolver, while the stage was rattling along as fast as the horses could haul it. The driver had fallen dead from the box, and a passenger who was upon the box was dying with a mortal wound. As soon as Paul could regain the lines that had fallen from the hands of Bud Philpot, who was shot through the heart, he drove and transferred Wells, Fargo & Co.'s box and the United States mail intact to J. D. Kinnear, the agent of the line at Benson, and the frightened passengers were sent through to Tombstone. Paul then started back, accompanied by four men, to the scene of the attack. Later particulars are awaited here with great interest.

"A vigilance committee was lately formed at Tombstone, backed by all the money necessary to take these parties in hand and teach them a lesson."[3]

According to Kate, the holdup during which driver Bud Philpot and a passenger were killed occurred during her second visit to Tombstone. "All I know about it is how Doc acted when he came home that afternoon," Kate later recalled. "Doc came home in a hurry. He said that he had particular work on hand and that he would not be able to take me to supper. About a half hour after he had left our room, Warren Earp [the youngest of the Earp brothers] came in with a note from Doc telling me to send him his rifle. I asked Warren why Doc wanted it, but Warren answered that he didn't know. Doc did not return to our room until late that night, and he did not bring his rifle. It was several days after the holdup before he returned it to the room."[4]

One of the four suspects in the stage robbery and the double killing was William Leonard, Doc's friend from Las Vegas. When Leonard relocated to southern Arizona he had fallen in with a bad crowd, abandoned his profession as a jeweler, and taken to robbing stages. Doc had paid his friend an early morning visit on March 15. Leonard was sharing a house two miles outside town with three men: Luther King, Harry Head, and Jim Crane. All of Leonard's roommates had dubious reputations. Doc stayed until four o'clock and then returned to Tombstone where he made himself comfortable at a gaming table at the Alhambra Saloon. He was

The main thoroughfare in Tombstone, Arizona, circa 1800 CHRIS ENSS

dealing faro when the news of the stage robbery reached him at eleven o'clock that evening.[5]

A posse made up of Bat Masterson, Virgil, Morgan, and Wyatt Earp, Wells Fargo agent Marshall Williams, and Robert Paul, shotgun messenger on the stage that was robbed, rode to the scene of the attack, but the robbers had fled. The men picked up the outlaws' trail and followed it. Three days after the robbery, Luther King was arrested on suspicion to commit robbery. King was encouraged to name his accomplices. They were Harry Head, Jim Crane, and William Leonard.[6]

It wasn't long before Doc was implicated in the crime. His friendship with Leonard and the recent visit to his home made him look suspicious. Doc reasoned the only way to clear his name was to capture those responsible and make them tell the truth. King was placed into custody at the Tombstone jail which had been left in the hands of an undersheriff, while

Gamblers enjoying a game of faro in Tombstone's Oriental Saloon CHRIS ENSS

the Earps and the rest of the posse continued with the search for the remaining stage robbers. Before Doc could question King, he escaped.[7]

A group of outlaw cowboys including well-known Cochise County, Arizona, residents Ike Clanton, Pete Spencer, Frank Stillwell, and Curly Bill Brocius encouraged the rumor of Doc Holliday's involvement in the robbery. An article in the March 24, 1881, edition of the *Arizona Weekly Citizen* implicated Doc in the crime as well. Three of the robbers were headed to Mexico. "The fourth is at Tombstone and is well-known and has been shadowed ever since his return." Doc was furious. Many suspected him of taking part in the robbery, and that included Kate.[8]

"I thought that after the holdup things looked very suspicious about the Earps and Doc," Kate recalled later. "Something tells me Doc was in with Wyatt, Virgil and Morgan in that affair. One night after we retired, Warren Earp came after Doc and said that Wyatt wanted to see him at his home. Doc was gone for almost two hours, and when he returned I could see that he was very much putout about something. He kept saying, 'the damned fool! I didn't think that of him.' And later he said, 'I have to get up early in the morning, but I will think about it.' This was after the holdup.

"In the morning, after we had our breakfast, Doc said, 'Well, I don't know what I am going to stack up against today. I am getting tired of it all.'"

Kate knew he was referring to the fact that several people believed he was one of the men who robbed the stage. She tried to convince Doc to leave town with her, but he refused. "Wyatt Earp had a powerful influence over Doc," Kate noted years later, "which I came to realize when I could not overcome that influence and induce Doc to return to Globe with me."[9]

By the beginning of April 1881, Kate had left Tombstone and traveled back to her business in Globe. Doc's troubles continued to mount. Shortly after Kate's departure, he was playing cards at the Oriental saloon when Milt Joyce, owner of the establishment, made a snide remark about Doc being a thief and murderer. The reference had to do with the stage robbery. Doc was outraged, and the two men argued. The fight was stopped before any shots were fired, but Joyce swore out a warrant for Doc's arrest, claiming Doc threatened his life. The charges against Doc were dropped after he paid a fine.[10]

The feud between Doc and Joyce continued into May. Joyce convinced his friend, Cochise County sheriff John Behan, to indict Doc on a felony charge for a shooting incident that had occurred in the fall of 1880. Doc was scheduled to appear in court in early June. He was in court every day he was ordered to be along with his attorney A.G.P. George. The matter was continued several times and eventually removed from the court schedule all together.[11]

According to Kate, Doc sent for her a second time after the matter between him and Joyce was put to rest on June 6, 1881. Doc invited Kate to spend Independence Day with him, and she happily accepted. Kate and Doc were reunited just before the holiday, but their time together was less than civil. His tuberculosis, which had been somewhat in remission while

Views of the copper mines in Globe, Arizona CHRIS ENSS

they were in New Mexico, was now causing coughing fits that brought up blood. To deal with the aggravation Doc drank to excess. Kate drank right along with him. The pair was not shy about arguing in public. The fight the couple had on July 4 ended in name-calling and cursing. Angry and crying, Kate staggered to the room she shared with Doc. The plan she had to sleep until she was no longer intoxicated was interrupted when John Behan and Milt Joyce stopped her before she reached the hotel.[12]

According to Kate, "Sheriff Johnny Behan took me to Judge Spicer's Justice of the Peace office, and the judge put me through the third degree. He asked me about the Earps and Doc Holliday. How did Doc act the evening of the holdup? Did the youngest or which one of the Earps came to me for Doc's rifle? Did Doc change his clothes that afternoon and what did Warren Earp say, if anything? How long had I known the Earps?

"Then suddenly he asked me, 'Are you sure that Doc Holliday was with the Earps at the holdup?'

"Then I told the judge I was positive of nothing and would not swear to anything Spicer said. He felt sure that the Earps and Holliday were in that holdup. I asked him why he did not question Mattie [Blaylock] and Alice Earp, that he knew Morgan Earp was the Wells Fargo messenger on that stage. The judge then got out of patients [sic] with me and threatened me. I said, 'I can't tell you anymore.'"[13]

Perhaps in her drunken state Kate did not recall signing an affidavit stating Doc had admitted to her he shot and killed the passenger and the driver of the stage that was robbed. Sheriff Behan presented the affidavit to the judge and was then given a directive to arrest Doc Holliday.

Kate still wasn't completely sober when she was arrested the afternoon of July 5. She was taken into custody for being drunk and disorderly. "After my session with Judge Spicer," Kate recalled years later, "Virgil Earp, who was city marshal of Tombstone by Mayor John P. Clum's appointment, arrested me and locked me in a room at the Bilicke Hotel. But before he got me there, I accused the Earps openly of pulling that holdup and killing Bud Philpot. I said, 'You are immune from punishment because of the official positions all of you hold in Tombstone.' 'That's all right, Kate,' Virgil replied, 'we'll fix that up some day.'"[14]

The Bilicke Hotel, where Kate was temporarily held, was an establishment owned by Albert Bilicke and known by most as the Cosmopolitan Hotel. Albert Bilicke and Wyatt were close friends. The pair had invested in a silver mining claim together and every courtesy was extended to Wyatt whenever he ventured into the business. While locked in one of the rooms at the Cosmopolitan, Kate had plenty of time to consider the allies the Earps had in town, what would happen to Doc, and her own contribution to his troubles. She had time to reflect on her life with Doc in New Mexico and how satisfied she was before the Earps came around. Even if she could make right what she'd done, what she and Doc once were could never be again.[15]

Kate wasted no time walking back any statements she might have made about Doc that implicated him in the stage robbery and death of two people. She insisted she was coerced into reporting anything negative about Doc. All murder charges against Doc were dismissed on July 9. The

Wyatt Earp COURTESY OF THE ARIZONA HISTORICAL SOCIETY, AHS 11374

judge reviewing the case determined there was no evidence to show Doc had a part in the crime.[16]

Kate planned to leave town as soon as she knew Doc was out of harm's way. She was aware she wasn't wanted in Tombstone. "It was after that," Kate noted later, referring to her arrest by Virgil Earp, "Wyatt Earp became anxious to get rid of me. Several days later [once she was released] a gambler named J. M. Nichols, also known as Napa Nick, invited me to go for a buggy ride with him, but I declined. Mattie Earp, Wyatt's wife, later told me in Globe that I was lucky in refusing the buggy ride, as Napa Nick had instructions to get rid of me in some lonely canyon."[17]

Reflecting on the turbulent and sad incident in her life years later, Kate confessed, "After the stage holdup Doc turned against me. I found out it was he who got Virgil Earp to lock me up in the hotel room. Wyatt and Virgil were doing all they could to get Doc to send me away, and no doubt they would have carried their point if I had let them.

"In order to block them I swore out a warrant charging Doc with murder and he was arrested by Sheriff Behan; and then Wyatt Earp and others of his gang furnished $5,000 bail to get him out. It took all the persecution of the Earps and all the law officers aligned with them to make me quit. In doing as I did I was taking a desperate chance, but I lost out."[18]

Kate returned to Globe and within a short time was faced with the difficult task of starting over. A fire claimed her boarding house and all her belongings. Kate suspected the fire was set intentionally by people hired to do the job for the Earps. She believed the fire was penance for her not keeping her "big nose" out of the Earps' business.[19]

While Kate was in Globe lamenting the great losses she'd experienced in a short amount of time, Doc remained in Tombstone trying to clear his name. Two of the men who had robbed the stage outside Benson had been seen in New Mexico Territory. Before Doc could enlist riders to help him track Bill Leonard and Harry Head to Eureka, New Mexico, the outlaws were shot and killed. Jim Crane was now the one and only thief who helped robbed the Arizona Mail Stage Company coach still alive. Doc wanted Crane found and made to tell the truth about the robbery.[20]

It was rumored that Crane had been seen with some of the cowboys from the Arizona Territory, namely, Ike Clanton and Frank McLaury. Wyatt Earp made a deal with Ike and Frank that if they told the law enforcement agent the whereabouts of Crane he would make sure they received the reward being offered for his arrest. Wyatt was informed that the criminal was last seen at the Clantons' ranch near Cloverdale, New Mexico. Wyatt, along with his brothers Morgan and Warren, and Doc Holliday started for the area right away. The posse found Crane in a canyon near Gillespie, New Mexico. He was with a handful of cowboys including Ike Clanton's father, Newman Haynes Clanton. In their possession was a herd of stolen cattle.[21]

The August 28, 1881, edition of the *Arizona Weekly Citizen* reported that the cattle rustlers were overtaken by either "Indians or Mexicans, but the general belief seems to be that the latter were the guilty parties." Newman Haynes Clanton, Jim Crane, and another cowboy were killed during the encounter.[22]

Tensions between the Earps, Holliday, Ike and Billy Clanton, along with the other cowboys, continued to increase. The Earps and Holliday were suspected of being the real gunmen who shot and killed Crane and the others in the so-called raid by the "Mexicans." Heated words were exchanged between the factions whenever their paths crossed in Tombstone. It wasn't a question of *if* but *when* the adversaries would square off against one another.[23]

Shortly after the violent incident in Gillespie, Doc left Tombstone for parts unknown. Sometime between late August and September 9, 1881, Kate and Doc reunited and traveled to Tucson to enjoy the annual festival to celebrate the city's patron saint, San Augustine. The event attracted people from all over the territory. Among those in attendance were ranchers, artists, gamblers, and enterprising businessmen—some of whom opened ice cream saloons to serve the public something cold and refreshing during the fiesta.[24]

After Kate and Doc had enjoyed more than a month of uninterrupted time, one of the Earps tracked the pair down at a popular saloon on Meyer Avenue in Tucson. According to Kate, on October 25, 1881, she was standing behind Doc watching him deal cards when again their lives were disrupted. "The day before the fight took place in Tombstone, Wyatt sent Morgan to Tucson to tell Doc that he was wanted in Tombstone the following day," Kate shared later. "Morgan found us at Congress Hall where Doc was trying his luck at [the] faro bank. He took Doc aside and delivered the message from Wyatt.[25]

"Then Doc came to me and told me that he would take me to our hotel, as he had to go back to Tombstone, but that he would come for me later on. I would not have it that way, though, and told him that if he was going to Tombstone I was going with him. We left on a freight for Benson and from there drove to Tombstone in a buckboard. Doc and I had a room in the building owned by Mr. and Mrs. Fly, who also had a photograph gallery there. It was on Fremont Street next to the back entrance of the O.K. Corral. We got to the room after midnight. Doc left me there, he and Morgan going away together."[26]

Doc and Morgan set off for the Alhambra Saloon where Wyatt was waiting for them. Wyatt informed Doc of the ongoing difficulties with Ike Clanton. Ike was remorseful that the information he had given Wyatt about Jim Crane's whereabouts had led to his father's death. He was furious with himself and Wyatt. He believed the lawman had shared with Doc the deal the two had struck, naming the location of Crane in exchange for money. Wyatt denied he ever discussed the matter with Doc, but Ike called him a liar and stormed off into the night to brood in anger. Wyatt told Doc what had transpired and warned him to be on his guard.[27]

Doc turned his attention to playing cards and drinking whiskey. He didn't give the matter much thought until he ran into Ike at the restaurant adjacent to the saloon. It was after one in the morning, and Doc was less than sober. He cursed at Ike which started a verbal sparring between the two. According to Ike Clanton, Doc called him a "damn son-of-a-bitch" and told him to "get his gun out." Ike indicated in his eyewitness account of the matters leading up to the street fight that he left the eatery after his encounter with Doc. He noted that Morgan was watching the pair verbally abuse one another and that Morgan had his hand on his pistol. Seeing he was outnumbered, he left the building knowing that war between the Earps, Holliday, and the cowboys was on the horizon.[28]

"Doc and Ike Clanton had some words in a restaurant," Kate recalled about the events of the first night she returned to Tombstone in late October 1881. "In the morning Ike Clanton came to Fly's photograph gallery with a Winchester rifle. Mrs. Fly told him that Doc was not there. Doc was not up yet. I went to our room and told Doc that Ike Clanton was outside looking for him and that he was armed. Doc said, 'If God lets me live long enough to get my clothes on, he shall see me.'

"With that he got up and dressed. On going out he said, 'I won't be here to take you to breakfast, so you had better go alone.' I didn't go to breakfast. I don't remember whether I ate anything or not that day.

"In a little more than a half an hour the shooting began. This lady-friend and I went to the side window, which faced the vacant lot. There was Ike Clanton, young Bill Clanton, Frank McLowry [sic], and his brother Tom on one side, Virgil, Wyatt, and Morgan Earp and Doc Holliday on the other. Before the first shot was fired Ike Clanton ran and lost his hat and left his young brother and the McLowry boys to fight it out.*

"I was at the side window looking on and saw the fight. Doc had a sawed-off shotgun. He fired one barrel, but after the first shot something went wrong. He threw the gun on the ground and finished the fight with his revolver. I saw him fall once. His hip had been grazed by a bullet. But he was on his feet again in an instant and continued to fire.

"Bill Clanton and the McLowry boys were killed. Morgan and Wyatt [she meant Virgil Earp] were wounded. It's foolish to think a cow 'rustler' gunman can come up to a city gunman in a gunfight. After the fight was over, Doc came to our room and sat on the side of the bed and cried and said, 'Oh, this is just awful—awful.' I asked, 'Are you hurt?' He said, 'No, I am not.' He pulled up his shirt. There was just a pale red streak about two inches long across his hip where the bullet had grazed him. After attending to the wound, he went out to see how Virgil and Wyatt [she meant Morgan this time] were getting along."[29]

---

*It's been argued that Kate couldn't possibly have witnessed the gunfight because early in the encounter Sheriff Behan grabbed Ike Clanton and pulled him into the front door. Kate's critics insist she would have seen that occur. According to Kate, she watched the gunfight from a side window looking out at the vacant lot. From where she stood, she couldn't have possibly seen Behan pull Ike into the building.

John Ringo

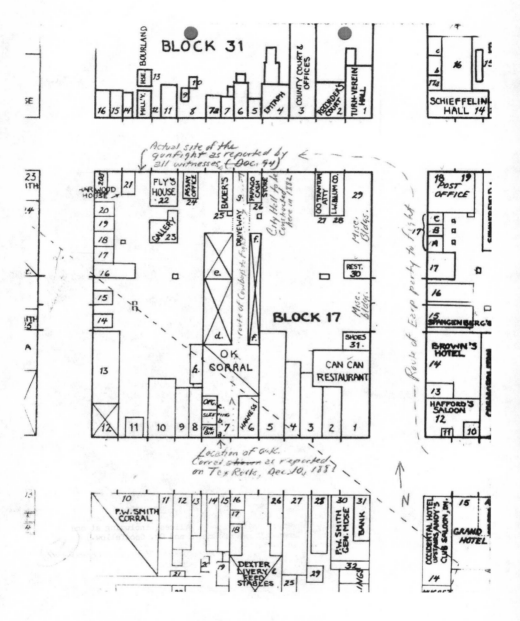

Map of the City of Tombstone and O.K. Corral location along with key to map
CHRIS ENSS

Bldg. 20   I   se
Bldg. 21   Cabin
Bldg. 22   Tombstone Livery, H. H. Tuttle
Bldg. 23   L. Graf, Blacksmith Shop
      24   Yard of Tombstone Livery surrounded by 4' adobe wall.
Bldg. 25   Blacksmith

Block 17:
Bldg. 1   Can Can Restaurant, Quong Kee, Prop.
Bldg. 2   Leigh Bros.
Bldg. 3   Moses & Mehan Saloon
Bldg. 4   D.R.N. Thompson Saddelry & Harness
Bldg. 5   Zeckendorf & Co.
Bldg. 6   Harness Room, OK Corral
Bldg. 7a   Tool Bin, OK Corral

Block 17 cont.
Bldg. 7b   Sleeping Area, OK Corral
Bldg. 7c   Office, OK Corral
Bldg. 7d   Barn, OK Corral
Bldg. 7e   Barn, OK Corral
Bldg. 7f   Covered Stalls, OK Corral
Bldg. 7g   North Entrance, OK Corral
Bldg. 7h   Lodging Rooms, OK Corral
            (Proprietors of OK Corral--John Montgomery & Edward Munroe Benson)

Bldg. 8   Dolan's Saloon
Bldg. 9   G. W. Bloor, Printing
Bldg. 10   Blacksmith
Bldg. 11   House, Mattie Webb
Bldg. 12   Sandy Bob Stage Barn
Bldg. 13   Sandy Bob Stage Corral
Bldg. 14   House
Bldg. 15   House
Bldg. 16   Harrington House
Bldg. 17, 18, 19 & 20   Houses
Bldg. 21   Harwood House
Bldg. 22   Camilus Fly Boarding House
Bldg. 23   "   "   Photography Gallery
Bldg. 24   Assay Office
Bldg. 25   A Bauer, Butcher Shop
Bldg. 26   Papago Cash Store
Bldg. 27   Office, O.O. Trantum, Atty.
Bldg. 28   I. W. Blum Co.
     (29)   Vacant lot, later site of Summerfield Dry Goods after summer '82.
Bldg. 30   Robert Campbell's Restaurant
Bldg. 31   Tappanier Shoe shop

Block 18:
Bldg. 1   Crystal Palace Saloon & Gambling (also known as Eagle Brewery
            Saloon at one time--located in the Wherfritz Bldg. Wherfritz
            ran Eagle Brewery. Upstairs were offices, including at one
            time Virgil Earp as Chief of Police and Dr. Goodfellow.)
Bldg. 1b.   Eagle Brewery in basement
Bldg. 2   Dave Cohen's Cigar Store (Where Behan offered Wyatt Job as Under-Sheriff)
Bldg. 3   Barber and Bath
Bldg. 3a   Nellgren & Nichols Saloon & Gambling
Bldg. 4   Wells, Fargo & Co. 1880 (later moved to S. side of Allen
            between 5th and 6th, still later to location of Safford and
            Hudson Bank after it failed in 1884)
Bldg. 5   Campbell & Hatch's Saloon and Billiard Parlor. (Morgan Earp
            killed here near back door while playing pool.)

6

Key to block 17 - map attached

2
3
4
5
6
7
8
9
10
11

6

12 EPITAPH OFFICE
13 COUNTY COURT & OFFICE
14 RECORDERS COURT
15 TURN-VEREIN HALL

16 SCHIEFFELIN HALL
17 POST OFFICE
18 SPANGENBERG'S GUN SHOP
19 BROWNS HOTEL
20 HAFFORDS SALOON
21 OCCIDENTAL HOTEL
22 BANK

On October 29, 1881, a coroner's inquest was held, and a summary of the evidence was compiled. Doc Holliday and the Earp brothers were charged with killing the McLaurys and Billy Clanton. Doc and Wyatt were confined to the county jail. A posse was recruited to guard the facility. Bail was set at more than $20,000. The two men were able to raise the necessary funds to be released.[30]

During the time the inquest was being conducted, Kate befriended an outlaw who was part of the group of cowboys Doc and the Earps had been warring against. The outlaw's name was Johnny Ringo. Ringo was a hard drinker who had been indicted for one murder and had been involved in several others. Kate remained in the room she and Doc shared at Fly's boarding house, and it was there that Ringo found her. Doc was residing at the Cosmopolitan Hotel while out on bail. Morgan and Virgil were staying at the Cosmopolitan recuperating, and their families were with them. Doc and Wyatt had decided to stay to protect them from any cowboys who might sneak in and try to kill the brothers.[31]

"I kept close to my room at Mrs. Fly's during the Earp-Holliday trial hearing before [the] justice of the peace," Kate recalled years later. "John Ringo visited me there twice. I gave him a tumble both times. The second time he advised me to leave the camp, but I told him I did not have enough money to go back to Globe as Doc had lost all my money playing against faro while we were in Tucson." Kate also noted in 1935 that she had a hundred dollars at the time of the gunfight at the O.K. Corral and gave seventy-five of it to help with Doc's bail.[32]

"Ringo said that some of the Clanton gang were watching for Doc to come to our room and intended to get him there," Kate added in her memoir. "Ringo told me 'if I haven't enough money here is fifty dollars.' So I left that evening.

"After the O.K. Corral fight, the Clanton and McLowry gang gave notice that they would get revenge on the Earps and Holliday. John P. Clum, who was mayor of Tombstone, was notified that he was on the list, and he left the camp. Virgil was the first they got. He was shot from ambush, but the bullet failed to reach a vital spot, but he was laid up some time with a shattered arm.

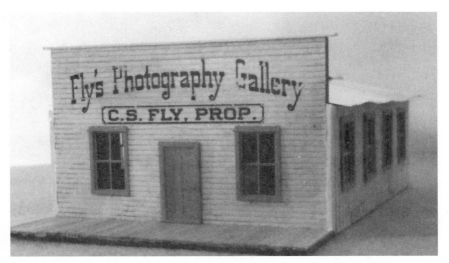

According to Kate, she watched the gunfight at the O.K. Corral from Fly's Photography Studio and Boarding House. CHRIS ENSS

"Morgan was the next victim. At the time he was playing pool in the Palace Saloon. The backdoor of the place was half-glass, painted white. Someone scratched off enough of the pain [sic] to see through and fired through the door, killing Morgan. I understand that the killer was one of the Clanton gang by [the] name of Stilwell."[33]

Kate left town in November 1881 before Doc's fate had been determined. She rebuilt her business in Globe and never again returned to Tombstone.[34]

Chapter Seven

Mrs. George Cummings

Kate Elder's hotel in the remote copper- and silver-mining town of Globe, Arizona, was a small, unassuming establishment that catered to prospectors, assayers, and occasionally outlaws. For twenty-five cents a night, guests were offered a clean room complete with a washbowl, towel, chamber pot, and a pitcher of fresh water. For an additional ten cents, Kate would provide breakfast. Patrons were served in the saloon in the front of the building, located a short distance from Alice Gulch, the site of the first silver claim.[1]

In late December 1881 a merchant named Mrs. Alonzo Bailey escorted a potential boarding house customer into the saloon where the last of the regular guests were finishing their morning meal. According to Kate, although it was past the time to serve food, the pair made themselves comfortable at a table and ordered coffee. The gentleman accompanying Mrs. Bailey was carrying a copy of the *Tombstone Epitaph*, and when Kate approached the duo with coffee cups and coffeepot, the man began to discuss the incident that had occurred at the O.K. Corral the previous month. "Some how Doc and I were mentioned," Kate noted when sharing the story with her niece several years later.[2]

Kate noted she didn't say a word about the happenings in Tombstone; she simply poured the coffee and went about the business of clearing the dishes. The chatty customer continued with his thoughts about the location of the gunfight and the people involved in the incident. "There are so many that claim they saw the shooting on Allen Street," Kate wrote her niece in March 1940, "It was not on Allen Street but nearer Freemont [sic] Street in an open lot."[3]

Kate ran a hotel in Globe, Arizona, called the Globe.

Kate invited Mrs. Bailey and her friend to help themselves to the bacon and eggs sitting on the buffet table near a stack of plates, forks, and knives. The man reluctantly set the newspaper aside to get a plate of food but never stopped talking. "He told Mrs. Bailey that Doc took me to New Mexico and killed me up in the mountains and that he helped to bury me," Kate recalled. "That poor woman," I remarked. "Mrs. Baily [sic] and I laughed but when the man found out he made a fool of himself he never came back. But it is laughable how some people will talk. I often laugh how often I have been dead and buried and turn up some place full of life."[4]

It's likely that Kate's business prospered in Globe. Mining companies such as the Old Dominion Mining Company merged with the Old Globe Copper Company, and together they became one of the greatest suppliers of copper ore in the region. The funds generated by the miners filtered into the community, and those businesses that provided miners, engineers, and managers with desired services benefited greatly. Kate's hotel and saloon did just that. There were periodic lulls in business, however. Globe was an extremely isolated area, a hundred miles from anywhere that could be considered civilization. Isolation bred outlawry. The proximity to the Apache Indian Reservation also invited trouble. In July 1882 a band of warring Apaches attacked ranches and mines in the area, forcing mercantiles, banks, and saloons to close their doors until the difficulty passed. Stages bringing new patrons to town were frequently robbed by bandits convinced what little law there was in Globe wouldn't dare stop them.[5]

Kate persevered despite the interruptions and managed to earn a healthy income. When she wasn't working, she followed the news in the papers about Doc Holliday's exploits with the Earps. Wyatt Earp and Doc Holliday appeared in court in November 1881 to testify as to what transpired at the gunfight. After four weeks of testimony, Justice Wells Spicer, who was trying the case, concluded that although Virgil Earp, as chief of police, "committed an injudicious and censurable act" in employing Doc, Wyatt, and Morgan to assist him in attempting to control the Clantons and McLaurys, he could attach no criminality to the unwise act. The judge deemed that neither Doc, Wyatt, nor Morgan should be convicted of any offense. The verdict infuriated the cowboys.[6]

"After the O.K. Corral fight, the Clanton and McLaury gang gave notice they would get revenge on the Earps and Holliday," Kate noted in her memoir. The night Morgan was being transported to Colton, California, to be buried, all four of the Earps and their wives went. The youngest Earp, Warren, was not married. Doc Holliday was with them. As the train got to Tucson, the Earps got a tip they were going to be taken in by some of the Clanton gang. Wyatt and Doc went through the train to the last car. They found two men there and shot them.

"This happened when Tucson was first lighted with gas. Everybody thought the shooting was in honor of the city being lighted. When the track-walker went on the track in the morning [March 20, 1882] he found two dead men, one of each side of the track.

"Doc and Wyatt did not go to Colton, they went back to Tombstone and stayed three days to settle some business."[7]

The business Doc and Wyatt had to settle was the vindication of Morgan's death and Virgil's life-altering injury. The March 24, 1882, edition of the *Record-Union* described the day they left Tombstone in search of justice.

"There was considerable excitement on the street yesterday," the article read, "occasioned by the departure from town of Wyatt Earp, Doc Holliday, Texas Jack and three of their retainers, whose names we did not learn. They rode up Allen Street, going east, while the sidewalks were crowded with throngs of citizens speculating upon their destination.

"Each of the horsemen was armed with a shotgun, Winchester rifle, and two revolvers, and at least a hundred rounds of ammunition. All sorts of rumors were rife upon the streets during the afternoon and evening, but until 6 o'clock no one knew to a certainty which direction, after leaving the city, the horsemen had taken. At that hour, however, a boy came in from Helm's ranch who stated he met the Earp party fifteen miles from town, riding hard in the direction of the ranch.

"About one and half miles behind the Earps was a company of fifteen to twenty cowboys, all heavily armed, riding furiously in pursuit, with every probability in favor of their soon coming up with a foremost party. If the boy's statements are true, and there seems no reason to doubt them, a bloody combat will surely be the result."[8]

Earp's vendetta ride ultimately led to the deaths of Curly Bill Brocius, Florence Cruz, and Johnny Barnes. In May 1882 Doc was arrested in Denver, Colorado, for the murder of Frank Stilwell. Released on bail, he traveled to Gunnison to reunite with Wyatt Earp. When Kate read the account of Doc's continued association with Wyatt, she noted in her memoir that she couldn't stop thinking about how she did her best to prevent Doc from joining them all those years ago but failed.[9]

While Doc was traveling the West as Wyatt Earp's most trusted friend and defender, Kate was spending time with many of the prominent male citizens of Globe. Among those was the future governor of Arizona, George W. P. Hunt. Hunt was waiting tables at local saloons for a time but was then hired as a clerk at a general store owned by the Old Dominion Mining Company. He eventually became the president of the mining concern and was then elected recorder for Gila County, Arizona. Judge A. H. Hackney, editor and founder of the Globe newspaper the *Arizona Silver Belt*, had also made Kate's acquaintances. Mayor A. H. Moreland and sawmill owner M. W. Breman were familiar with Kate, her hotel, and saloon as well.[10]

The last news Kate heard about Doc was that he was in Leadville, Colorado, and on trial for shooting a bartender named Billy Allen. "They arrested him and telegraphed to Tombstone that they had Doc Holliday," Kate recalled years later. "A deputy from Tombstone was sent for him with a requisition. Governor Tabor of Colorado refused to sign the document and told the Arizona deputy that Doc Holliday was too good a man to turn over to the Arizona cow thieves. He would not sign the requisition. Doc was free."[11]

Doc was eventually acquitted and moved to Denver. Kate received a letter from Doc in April 1887. He had plans to travel to Glenwood Springs and wanted her to meet him there. Kate couldn't refuse the invitation.[12]

"Holliday at last broke away from the Earps at Gunnison," Kate wrote years later. "A [chain] mail shirt was the cause of their parting company. Wyatt had a job to pull and was going to wear the mail shirt. But Doc said to Wyatt, 'No, you don't. If you want me to go into anything with you, you have to take the same chance I do or else we quit right here. I thought you had got rid of that shirt long ago.'"

"Wyatt insisted on wearing the mail shirt, so Doc left that evening and hit the trail for Leadville. But it was too cold for him, and he went from there to Denver, and later to Glenwood Springs. All those places were in Colorado."[13]

Kate and Doc reunited in Glenwood Springs in May 1887. Doc's health had substantially deteriorated. The disease that had been in remission for a time was now fully awake and eating his lungs from the inside out. His lungs were now mostly engulfed in liquid and sloshing around in his chest. Doc struggled to breathe and coughed all the time. Kate

---

*Kate doesn't mention exactly what the "job" was to which Wyatt Earp was referring. In her talks with Anton Mazzanovich she tells that Wyatt Earp "always had all manners of disguises, false mustaches, beards, and wigs of different shades." She infers that the disguises were used for nefarious reasons. The "mail shirt" is commonly known as a chainmail shirt. A chainmail shirt is a type of armor consisting of small metal rings linked together in a pattern to form a mesh.

noted in her memoir that when he arrived in the area he had tried to return to dentistry to support himself, but the persistent cough made the work impossible to do. Doc then took a short-term job guarding a mining claim for a well-known prospector. According to Kate, Doc also served as "Under Sheriff of Garfield County under Sheriff Ware."[14]

Prior to traveling to Colorado, Kate had become reacquainted with her brother Alexander Horony, who was living in Penny Hot Springs, twenty-nine miles from Glenwood Springs. The area was named for the naturally hot mineral water that fed into the many primitive rock pools. They were a rich source of sulfur, and their healing benefits included treating infections and digestive disorders. Kate convinced Doc to go with her to visit her brother and to take advantage of healing properties in the springs around Alexander's home. Kate and her sister-in-law saw to it Doc got plenty of rest and maintained a diet of mostly vegetables and fish. Nothing they did could reverse the effects of tuberculosis that had ravaged Doc's being. Kate escorted the frail Doc Holliday back to Glenwood Springs where the pair registered in separate rooms at the Hotel Glenwood. Doc gambled some and occasionally won a few dollars that helped

Hotel Glenwood, where Doc Holliday passed away on November 8, 1887
CHRIS ENSS

Kate's brother's home in Red Rock, Colorado CHRIS ENSS

pay for necessities, but the couple was sustained primarily on money Kate had saved.[15]

Doc Holliday passed away November 8, 1887, at ten o'clock in the morning.[16]

"I nursed him and attended to his affairs until he died," Kate remembered years later. "His last words were, 'Well, I'm going just as I told them—the bugs would get me before the worms.' He was buried by the gamblers and had the biggest funeral ever given a Colorado gambler. The whole town turned out to it."[17]

Doc Holliday's death was reported in many newspapers throughout the West including the December 14, 1887, edition of the *Helena Independent*. An article entitled "Death of a Notorious Bunco Man" described the life Doc had lived and the trouble he had encountered.[18]

"Few men have been known to a certain class of sporting people, and few men of character had more friends or stronger champions. He represented a class of men who are fast disappearing in the new West. He had the reputation of being a bunco man, desperado, and bad man generally, yet he was a very mild-mannered man, was genial and companionable and had many excellent qualities.

"In Arizona he was connected with the Wyatt Earp gang. These men were officers of the law and were opposed to the 'rustlers' or cattle thieves. Holliday killed several men during his life in Arizona and his body was full of wounds received in bloody encounters.

"His history was an interesting one. He was sometimes in the right, but quite often in the wrong in his various escapades. The doctor had only one deadly encounter in Colorado. This was in Leadville. He was well-known in Denver and had lived here a good deal in the past few years. He had strong friends in some old-time detective officers and in certain representatives of the sporting element.

"He was rather a good-looking man, and his coolness and courage, his affable ways and fund of interesting experiences, won him many admirers. He was a strong character. He had been well-known to all the states and territories west of Kentucky."[19]

John Henry Holliday's grave in Glenwood Springs, Colorado CHRIS ENSS

Not long after Doc was laid to rest, Kate left Glenwood Springs. She remained in Colorado, however, traveling to the popular mining community of Carbondale, thirteen miles from her brother's home. Doc had been a constant in her life for more than fifteen years. The thought of not seeing him ever again filled her with grief, and she sought to drown her sorrows in a bustling community where no one knew of her past or of the unhappy memories she was leaving behind.[20]

Carbondale and the other towns in Garfield County reminded Kate of Globe. Gold and silver miners who had staked out claims in the area congregated in Carbondale to cash in their finds and gather supplies. In addition to the prospectors, the town was busy with farmers and hunters who raised bountiful crops in the rich, fertile river-bottom land and lived off the elk, mule deer, and bear they tracked and killed. Cattle and sheep ranches were in abundance too.[21]

Kate doesn't mention what she did to earn a living in Carbondale. She was hoping for a fresh start and a respectable line of work. It's conceivable she gained employment operating a boarding house, one strictly in the business of offering rooms to a more genteel clientele looking for more than a one- or two-night stay. She stopped using the name Kate Elder and referred to herself as Mary Horony.[22]

In 1888 Kate met George M. Cummings. He was a popular mine owner and the marshal of Carbondale. The *Aspen Evening Chronicle* noted that George was accomplished in many areas with "a talent most profound for finding rich ore." George worked a claim called Rock Creek, ten miles north of Carbondale. The September 14, 1888, edition of the *Aspen Evening Chronicle* reported on George's unearthing of the Cumming's Mine in Conundrum Gulch in 1881 and his subsequent finds. "Recently Cummings discovered a vein of rich ore within fifty feet of the old trail where the wagon now runs through Rock Springs," the article began. "A few weeks ago, he shipped a mill run of two hundred twenty pounds from which he received the handsome sum of $224. There are immense quantities of good concentrated ores here as well as rich ones."[23]

George was well-known in mining camps from Bailey Mountain to Carbondale. He had a reputation for being a "good bear hunter" and "a friendly drinker." Kate must have been as well-known in the area, too,

Kate moved to Carbondale, Colorado, after the death of Doc Holliday.
THE DENVER PUBLIC LIBRARY, WESTERN HISTORY COLLECTION, X-6784

because when the pair announced their engagement in the January 8, 1890, edition of the *Carbondale Avalanche*, she was referred to quite favorably. "The marriage of George Cummings to one of Carbondale's best girls is listed for March," the article read. "George, we wish you luck and hope you will put the management of your affairs in your wife's hands, and then we will be able to get a straight item once in a while."[24]

Kate Elder, now Mary Horony, wedded George Cummings on March 2, 1890. The local newspaper lamented the fact that another Carbondale bachelor had taken the plunge. "Good Lord!" an article about George and Kate getting married in the March 5, 1890, edition of the *Carbondale Avalanche* began. "The marrying craze seems to have struck this neck of the woods worse than the la grippe. Al Johnson, Ed Gift, George Cummings and the Lord only knows how soon Bill Dinkel, John Turner, Ed Cook, Holmes, and a whole lot of other miserable, old bachelors will catch the contagion."[25]

The Cummingses resided in Garfield County, Colorado, for more than five years after they wedded. George supported the pair by leasing the various mining claims he had and as a law enforcement agent. Mr. and Mrs. Cummings left Colorado in 1895 and moved to Bisbee, Arizona. Bisbee was reminiscent of other mining towns where the two had lived and worked. The Mule Mountains that surrounded the southern Arizona town contained lead, silver, and copper. A multitude of prospectors hurried to the area in hopes of striking it rich. Numerous ore bodies had been uncovered, and Bisbee was known as the "Queen of the Copper Camps."[26]

Kate and George had no trouble settling in Bisbee. They made friends quickly, and George partnered with some of those friends in a search for his own claim. He hoped to duplicate the success he'd had in Colorado, but when it seemed he'd never make an important find again he began drinking. George's drinking escalated and became a serious problem in his marriage. Kate tolerated the situation for a time and in 1893 decided a move was in order. The couple retreated to the town of Pearce, fifty-three miles north of Bisbee. Gold had been discovered there in 1894, silver in 1895. Kate thought George might have better luck prospecting around Pearce and that a change in fortune would curb his drinking.[27]

When George wasn't searching for copper, silver, or gold, he was employed as a blacksmith at a mine operated by Percy Clark. Kate was hired as a cook at one of the local eateries. Pearce was a thriving town with several stores, restaurants, saloons, and boarding houses. Town allotments were selling at one dollar a foot.[28] Kate wanted to purchase a couple hundred allotments and build a house she and George could share. George didn't care for the idea. He liked prospecting and the ability to move on to the next boom town uninhibited. George's drinking continued to be an issue, and that, combined with his unwillingness to stay in one area for

Kate relocated to Bisbee, Arizona, in 1895 with her husband, George Cummings.
CHRIS ENSS

an extended period, contributed to the end of his marriage to Kate. The couple parted ways in 1899.[29]

George drifted around mining camps near Globe and Prescott before returning to Colorado. He resumed prospecting in Aspen and was hired again as a law enforcement agent in Carbondale. By 1915 he was back in Arizona and living in the thriving mining camp of Courtland. George struggled with cancer and on July 7, 1915, took his own life.[30]

In 1899 Kate Elder turned forty-nine years old. She was divorced and a woman with a colorful past and an uncertain future. At this point in her life, few in her immediate sphere of influence knew she was once Doc Holliday's paramour. They didn't know her as Kate Elder or Big Nose Kate, and she seldom volunteered any information about her life prior to marrying George Cummings. Occasionally, a newspaper article about her time with Doc would surface, and she would pore over the story with fondness and frustration. Although she affectionately remembered the times she had with the gambler dentist she referred to as her husband, she was annoyed that what history recalled of the couple was tied to the Earps. One such article appeared in the November 4, 1896, edition of the *Fort Wayne Sentinel*.

"In Tombstone, Arizona, in 1879, there existed a gang of outlaws that refused to be broken up for years," the *Fort Wayne Sentinel* article read. "Wyatt Earp, who had been the marshal of Dodge City, resigned his position and went with the rush to Tombstone. In the party with which Wyatt made the journey was Doc Holliday and Big Nose Kate.

"Holliday was a good fellow, but one day caught Ed Bailey monkeying with the deadwood during a game of poker, and as a gentle reminder ran a knife between Bailey's ribs in the neighborhood of his heart. For this little thing he was arrested, but through the cunning of Big Nose Kate managed to escape.

"While the officers sat in front of the hotel with their prisoner, Kate set fire to the barn and cried 'fire!' Everybody ran to the rear, when Kate hurried to the front and covered the officers with revolvers. Doc and Kate backed from the room and made their escape and finally located in Tombstone. The town had taken on a boom and thieves and robbers were numerous. Wyatt was, after much persuasion, induced to become the marshal of Tombstone. Wyatt and his brothers saved the town from the outlaws who were once the terror of the border."[31]

In mid-1899 Kate packed her belongings and memories and left the Sulphur Springs Valley of Cochise County, Arizona, heading northwest.

CHAPTER EIGHT

Life in Dos Cabezas

KATE ELDER ARRIVED IN THE TOWN OF COCHISE STATION IN LATE 1898.
Cochise Station, located fifty-five miles from Tombstone, was on the
Southern Pacific Railroad line and situated between Willcox, Arizona,
and the Dragoon Summit. Named after the Chiricahua Apache chief
Cochise, the town was established in 1882. At its peak, Cochise Station
had a population of more than three thousand people. Cowboys shipping
their cattle East, miners transporting their ore, railroad employees seeking
to expand the line, and east- and westbound passengers congregated in
the burgeoning whistle-stop. Kate found work in Cochise Station at the
Rath Hotel. Owned by Lulu and John Rath, the hotel not only offered
a comfortable place for people to stay, but also served as the Wells Fargo
office, telegraph office, post office, and restaurant. Kate's job at the hotel
was that of housekeeper.[1]

It wasn't until after Kate was hired at the Rath Hotel that she learned
of her employer's association with the cowboys—the group of outlaws
that had crossed paths with the Earps and Doc Holliday in 1881. Lulu
was related to a rustler named Joe Hill, also known as Joe Olney. He
was a friend of the Clantons and McLaurys. Ike Clanton had sent Hill
to the location where the men who robbed the Benson stage and killed
Bud Philpot were hiding. The stage holdup and murders had been the
crimes Kate had suggested Doc had taken part in. Hill, along with Ike,
Frank, and Tom McLaury, later threatened the lives of Wyatt, Morgan,
and Virgil Earp, and Doc Holliday. Kate believed if the Raths learned
her true identity they might make trouble. Even after so many years had
passed, the hatred the cowboys and the descendants of the cowboys had

for the Earps, Holliday, and anyone who knew or were involved with them continued.[2]

On September 9, 1899, the westbound Southern Pacific train was held up about midnight at Cochise Station. The September 11, 1899, edition of the *Arizona Republic* reported that the Wells Fargo and Company safe in the express box was blown open and most of the contents rifled by two robbers who escaped. "The booty is reported to be considerable," the article noted. "The hold-ups did not go through the passenger cars and nobody was hurt. The train coming from the south stopped at the station as usual, and Charles Adair, the Wells Fargo and Company's messenger, opened the door of the express car to throw out the box. Two masked men approached him, ordering him to throw up his hands. He complied and walked with the men to the front end of the train where the engineer and fireman were forced to come out of the cab and walk back to the express car.[3]

"There is strong suspicion that the masked men were not the only two interested in the holdup. Two or three men stood around the station while the fireman was engaged in uncoupling the cars. They made no attempt to get away, nor did they get involved in the operations, but seemed stationed and ready to take part if necessary."[4]

The robbers got away on horses stationed near the Rath Hotel. Authorities believed the two men who planned such a smooth robbery probably had assistance, and there were some in Cochise Station that believed Kate might have been involved. The proximity of the horses to the hotel prompted the sheriff and his deputies to suspect someone at the establishment, either a guest or employee, had made sure the horses were in place. The Raths were considered beyond reproach. John was, in fact, the justice of the peace. According to Kate, "a number of train hold-ups, successful and otherwise, had occurred in the last year or two between Cochise and the New Mexico line, and many of those freebooters were still on the run. The Black Jacks, Cyclone Bills, Climax Jims and others. I wasn't as well-known as the others in town, and the law was desperate. In time they thought different of me."[5]

Whether Kate was fired from her job at the hotel or she simply decided it was in her best interest to find work elsewhere isn't known. She

Dos Cabezas, Arizona, was Kate Elder's home for many years. CHRIS ENSS

Kate Elder and John Howard spent time at the community hall in Dos Cabezas along with many other town residents. CHRIS ENSS

noted in her memoir that the Rath Hotel was going to close and that she needed to find work elsewhere. There were rumors that Kate didn't get along with Lulu Rath or her daughters and that she was in danger of having her position terminated. Kate recalled that Lulu presented her with an advertisement posted in the *Tucson Citizen* by a man in desperate need of a housekeeper. She took that as proof Lulu wanted her gone. By June 1900 Kate had relocated to a nearby mining camp and was working for a profitable prospector.[6]

An incident that occurred a month after Kate left her position at the Rath Hotel made her pleased she'd moved when she did. Residents of the town might have thought Mary Cummings incapable of being anything other than the unassuming housekeeper at the Rath Hotel, but as Big Nose Kate Elder they would surely believe her capable of any sordid illegal business possible—even murder.[7]

On July 6, 1900, Warren Earp, youngest of the four Earp brothers, was shot through the heart at a Willcox eatery by cowboy Johnny Boyett. The shooting occurred early in the morning and had grown from a feud that had existed between the two men ever since the bloody fights

Now known as the Cochise Hotel, Kate Elder worked there when it was the Rath Hotel. CHRIS ENSS

between the Earps and Arizona cattle rustlers around Tombstone in the early 1880s. The July 9, 1900, edition of the *San Francisco Chronicle* noted that Earp had for months habitually bullied Boyett and that Boyett had always tried to avoid a quarrel. "A few days ago Earp cornered Boyett in a saloon, and pressed a revolver against Boyett's stomach," the article read, "and made him promise that if they ever quarreled again that the one should kill the other.

"The two men met in a restaurant and Earp began his abuse. Boyett went into an adjoining saloon, followed by Earp. The latter said, 'Boyett, go get your gun and we'll settle the matter right here. I've got my gun; go get yours.' Boyett was willing and agreed to return in a few moments and fight it out. Earp also left the saloon. Boyett returned very soon and finding Earp gone warned all loungers in the saloon to clear out emphasizing his warning by shooting into the ceiling. Earp shortly appeared through a back door. He started toward Boyett, throwing open his coat and saying, 'Boyett, I am unarmed; you have all the best of this,' advancing as he spoke. Boyett warned him not to come nearer, but Earp did not heed the words, and within eight feet Boyett fired shooting Earp through the heart and killing him instantly."[8]

On July 13, 1900, Boyett was arrested and charged with the killing of Warren Earp. A preliminary hearing was quickly set. In late July 1900

Virgil Earp left his ranch in Kirkland, Arizona, to travel to Willcox to visit his brother's grave. Warren had been buried at the Willcox cemetery. Boyett was afraid Wyatt would join Virgil in Willcox and seek to avenge the death of Warren the same way he avenged Morgan's killing, but nothing like that took place. Virgil did, however, ride through the surrounding area to witness firsthand the growth in the territory.[9]

According to Kate, Virgil stopped in Cochise Station and had a meal at the Rath Hotel. Kate was certain if Virgil had seen and recognized her he would have made trouble for her. She believed he might even have gone so far as to suggest she conspired with John Boyett to kill Warren. Kate stayed out of Cochise Station until Virgil rode out of town. Boyett was eventually tried for shooting Warren and found innocent on the grounds that he acted in self-defense.[10]

When Kate left Cochise Station, she moved to Dos Cabezas to work for John Jesse Howard. She made twenty dollars a month as his housekeeper, and room and board were included. Dos Cabezas was situated high above the Sulphur Springs Valley. In the 1880s it had been the battleground of the Apache Indians and the ranchers, miners, and settlers in southern Arizona. Prospectors found copper, silver, and gold at the site, and miners with considerable funds hurried to the camp with workers and began digging a tunnel to the riches. John Howard was one of those miners who had found some of the riches in Dos Cabezas and lived in hope of finding much more.[11]

Born in England in 1845, Howard had come to the United States in 1854. He was divorced and, according to Kate, an overly cautious man. He refused to add a door to the outhouse on the off chance someone might sneak onto his property and try to overtake him. He used the facility with a Winchester in hand, ready to defend what was his. In addition to his many mining interests, Howard made and sharpened tools for the prospectors and mining companies in the area. Historical records on hand at the Arizona Historical Society note that Howard was a contentious individual, unafraid to take neighbors to task for encroaching on his property. He was a well-respected figure in Dos Cabezas, and Howard Peak and Howard Canyon were named for him.[12]

There's no indication that Howard's wife lived with him at Dos Cabezas, but he did spend time with her outside town. An article in the February 7, 1907, edition of the *Bisbee Daily Review* reported that the couple vacationed in Tombstone for the month. Howard explained to a reporter for the paper that Dos Cabezas was flourishing. "There's more men working in the district than has been in a number of years. Regular shipments of ore are being made to Willcox and the long-range outlook for the camp is exceedingly bright."[13]

Kate and John were two of the more than eight hundred people living in the camp built on the side of a canyon. Homes there rose in terraces, one above the other. The community was isolated from amusement, so they made their own, some in which Kate most assuredly participated. Dos Cabezas had a community hall where church services, dances, and all other camp functions were held.[14]

The community house operated as a club with a board of directors made up of miners and mine owners. The members, including John Howard, paid dues of two dollars per month, and the dances and all other entertainment were free of charge.[15]

Besides the community house, there were two schools for the children of the camp. There was also a barber shop, a brewery, a general store, brickyard, three saloons, a hotel, and a blacksmith shop. Kate was content in Dos Cabezas and with the living arrangement she had with Howard. Not only did she perform a number of household duties, but she also tended the garden and fruit orchard as well as fed the chickens. Gone were the days when Kate dressed in lavish garments suited for a woman who spent time entertaining men at saloons and dance halls. She now wore long, black dresses, and those who knew of her in Dos Cabezas noted she walked partially stooped over as a result of osteoporosis.[16]

The April 26, 1906, edition of the *Arizona Republican* included an article that noted that the Dos Cabezas "foothills and vicinity was covered with prospectors and a number of men in the gulches were working placer diggings and making good wages at it." As a former soiled dove, and well beyond the years to entertain the notion of reentering the profession, it's likely that Kate reflected on her time working in similar boomtowns. Sporting women had the potential to make a substantial amount of money off the men who frequented such camps as Dos Cabezas. The income gave soiled doves the feeling they were in charge of their destiny. Some ladies of joy just wanted to make enough money to live respectably. Some were part-time entertainers hoping to strike it rich, and others, of course, were just mercenaries. Kate was not one of those who had made enough money in the business to retire. In 1910, at the age of sixty, Kate was living a quiet, upright life earning a modest sum with nothing to put away for the days to come. The only company she now entertained was her brother and his wife when they traveled from Colorado to visit.[17]

Kate Elder was in the past—so, too, was the time for sporting women, even in places like Dos Cabezas. In the United States, the social purity movement was on the rise, and advocates for women's rights held that prostitution in any form was an exploitation of women and male dominance over women. It was argued that prostitution had a negative effect both on the prostitute and on society. Women like Kate had lived their lives as though they were in complete disagreement with that position. They believed that prostitution was a valid choice for women and men who choose to engage in it.[18]

The 1910 census listed Kate's occupation as servant.[19] More than thirty years prior, her occupation had been listed as prostitute. That was another life to Kate now. She was far removed from any of the ties that bound her to the road she used to travel and wanted to keep it that way. Occasionally, however, there were people with whom Kate came in contact that reminded her of the way things used to be. Her employer, John Howard, was friends with another Dos Cabezas resident named William "Major" Downing. Downing was rumored to have been the one who killed cowboy Johnny Ringo. Downing's young daughter, Delia, had been romantically involved with Ringo. The protective father tracked Ringo and shot him in the head. Downing's widow, Ellen, often visited Howard's home, where she and John would discuss Downing and Ringo.[20] According to Kate, the conversation made her uncomfortable. Ringo had been found dead at Morse Canyon in the Chihuahua Mountains on July 14, 1882, less than nine months after Kate had left Tombstone with the

Eighty-year-old Kate Elder (center) surrounded by family
COURTESY OF SHARLOT HALL MUSEUM LIBRARY AND ARCHIVES C-130 ITEM 4 FOLDER 1 BOX 7

money he had given her. The July 18, 1882, edition of the *Los Angeles Times* reported that Ringo committed suicide. Kate shared nothing of her association with Ringo to Howard.[21]

John Howard and Kate did confide in one another about matters unrelated to the history of the area. Howard's marriage to Mary Alvira Vanderwalker was a difficult one. The pair separated in the early 1900s and eventually divorced. Mary then moved to Bisbee with their twin daughters, Jessie and Dessie. John noted in his will that the last time he had seen his children was in the fall of 1898. He [had] met the nine-year-old girls on their way to school in Dos Cabezas. "After giving them candy," Howard wrote, "Jessie said 'Come on, Dessie. Don't let anyone see us talking to him.'" The twins hurried off, and that was the last Howard ever spoke to them. For years Kate encouraged Howard to reach out to the twins to try and reconcile things. In 1910 he wrote a letter to Jessie who was married by that time and living near San Francisco. He never received an answer. "I gave up the idea of reconciliation on August 7, 1920," Howard noted in his will. "I received a letter from Mrs. Dessie Lemelle, Dessie Howard. This is the first and only letter I received from them which is full of hatred and shall be enclosed with my will."[22]

Although attempts to restore relations with his children were unsuccessful, Howard was grateful to Kate for urging him to make an effort. He expressed his gratitude after his death in January 1930. Howard named Kate the executrix of his estate and left her his homestead, the Adriatic Group of mines, mining tools, books, notes, and documents. He left his daughters five dollars each. Kate sent the funds along, but they were returned.[23]

Kate was nearly eighty years old when John Howard died. Neighbors recalled how she walked to their home early on the morning he passed away. Kate was crying. "Jack died last night and I sat up all night with him," she explained. "Will you please come over and help me?" Mining operations had declined two years prior to his death. The local population dwindled, and the railroad operations were suspended and dismantled. Given the economic climate, the property Kate inherited was worth very little. She sold what she could for a small sum and traveled to Colorado to visit her brother. She returned to Dos Cabezas in October 1930 and rented a room from a family in town.[24]

By Christmas 1930 Kate was destitute and without a home of her own.[25]

Chapter Nine

The Pioneers' Home

"Pardon me for writing these few lines," Kate's letter to Arizona governor George W. P. Hunt, dated July 29, 1931, began. "I haven't a dollar and no where to go. My rent is due. All I have is what the [they] furnish to eat. I have to pay rent, buy wood—no money to do it with.

"I've sent my application [to] secretary [sic] of State Institutions Mr. Zander [and] he answered that [when a] vacancy occurs he will take care of me. If this vacancy does not occur soon; Is there no place for me; I am nearing my eighty-first year. I am not able to work at present. I am a county ward as I wrote you when I sent in my application to you some time last spring.

"Please, Mr. Hunt, if it is in your power help me out, see that I am admitted to the pioneer home. My application was signed by his honor our Superior Judge John W. Rose.

"Please, Mr. Hunt, help me to be admitted to the pioneer home.

"I remain most respectfully, Mrs. Mary K. Cummings."[1]

Since Kate's longtime employer John Howard had passed away in January 1930, she had struggled to make it on her own. Although Howard had left her his homestead, mining claims, and personal belongings, the property was virtually worthless. The riches in the hills around Dos Cabezas had nearly played out, and many people had moved away. Kate didn't have the funds to maintain the home or to purchase wood to keep warm.[2]

In April 1930 she had written to C. M. Zander, secretary of the Board of Directors of State Institutions, requesting he help her find a place to

STATE OF ARIZONA—BOARD OF DIRECTORS OF STATE INSTITUTIONS

FRIEND'S CERTIFICATE

STATE OF ARIZONA)
)ss.
County of _Cochise_)

BOYER COLLECTION

I, _Edwin N White_, being first duly sworn, depose and say that I know _Mary K Cummings_; that he is _80_ years of age; that he has resided in Arizona continuously _35_ years; that he uses or has used alcohol or drugs only moderately; that he is a person of good character and has been active in the development of Arizona, and that he is unable to properly provide himself with the necessary and ordinary comforts of life.

Edwin N White
Signature.

Subscribed and sworn to before me this _31st_ day of _Jan._, A. D. 193_1_.

My commission expires _July 18-1932_   _C A Anderson_
(SEAL)   Notary Public.

PHYSICIAN'S CERTIFICATE

Jan 31, Date   Town _Willcox_, County _Cochise_

I have this day examined _Mrs Mary K Cummings_, and find the following conditions: _Feble + hard of hearing_

Contagious or infectious disease? _None_

Suffering from an acute or chronic disease or ailment? _No except deafness_

Alcohol or drug habit? _No_

B. E. Briscoe M. D.
Signature.

STATE OF ARIZONA)
)ss.
County of _Cochise_)

BOYER COLLECTION

I, _Dr. B. E. Briscoe_, being first duly sworn, depose and say that the foregoing statement is true and correct to affiant's own knowledge.

Subscribed and sworn to before me this _31st_ day of _January_, A. D. 193_1_.

My commission expires _July 18,1932._   _C A Anderson_
(SEAL)   Notary Public.

RULES FOR THE PIONEERS' HOME

NOTE—Upon the first violation of any of these rules, the authorities of the county from which the member of the Home is admitted will be notified. A second infringement will result in a thirty-day enforced furlough, and a third offense will be punished by dismissal from the Home.

1. Men requiring continual care by reason of insanity or imbecility will not be admitted to the Home, because no provisions have been made for the care of such persons.

2. Profane or obscene language is forbidden in the buildings or on the grounds.

3. Scrupulous cleanliness in person, dress, and in quarters is positively enjoined. All members will be required to bathe at least once a week.

4. No loud, boisterous, or angry discussions on any subject will be allowed.

5. Due regard for the rights of other members and respectful demeanor to the officers and management of the Home must be maintained.

6. Waste or defacement of the property and utilities of the Home will not be permitted.

7. The Superintendent may make details from among the members for such duties as he may deem necessary for the general welfare of the Home.

8. All members of the Home will be required to conduct themselves at all times, whether in the Home or out of it, in a gentlemanly manner.

9. Leaves of absence may be granted to the members of the Home by the Superintendent whenever he may deem it neecssary. Members absent without above permission will be discharged.

10. Smoking will be permitted only in the rooms in the building designated by the Superintendent.

11. Complaints of neglect or ill treatment must be made in writing to the Board of Directors of State Institutions through the Superintendent. It shall be the duty of the Superintendent to at once forward such complaints to the Board.

12. The use of intoxicating liquors on the grounds or in the buildings is prohibited, except when prescribed by the physician of the Home. Any member bringing liquor of any kind on the grounds or into the buildings will be liable to immediate discharge. No excuse will be accepted for a violation of this rule.

13. Members are prohibited to have fire arms in their possession, or in the building or on the grounds. Members violating this rule will be discharged.

14. Use of any drug, except when prescribed by the physician of the Home, disobedience of orders, or refusal to perform any labor or duty imposed, when physically able, will render any member liable to summary discharge.

If admitted to the Home, I promise to abide by the above rules.

Signed _Mrs. Mary K. Cummings._

THE ARIZONA PRINTERS, INC.

Kate Elder's Application for Admission to the Pioneers' Home
CHRIS ENSS

live. She corresponded with him often, each time describing her desperate situation. In a letter dated August 24, 1930, Kate announced she had been hospitalized.[3]

"Dear Mr. Zander, I am writing to advise you that I am here in the C.C. hospital [Cochise County Hospital] for treatment for a sore foot. I was stung last summer by some poisonous insict [sic], but that [is] not the only reason I am here, the main reason is, I want to save money to pay my fare to the pioneer and some over.

"So when there is a vacancy you will know where to write mi [sic].

"Respectfully, Mrs. Mary K. Cummings. P. S. I am writing sitting on a chair, not a wheelchair. MKC"[4]

The "pioneer home" Kate was referring to was the Arizona Pioneers' Home, also known as the Home for Arizona Pioneers and State Hospital for Disabled Miners, located in Prescott, Arizona. The three-story retirement home had opened on February 11, 1911. The home could initially accommodate forty men. It was open to destitute men who were at least sixty years old and who had been living in Arizona for twenty-five years. In 1916 an addition was built to accommodate twenty women. Among some of the well-known Arizona pioneers living at the home in 1930 were Edward McGinley, the oldest prospector in Arizona, and

Pioneers' Home in Prescott, Arizona CHRIS ENSS

Bob Heckle, a scout in the army of famed Arizona Apache Indian fighter General George Crook.[5]

According to Kate, she had gone through the proper channels to gain admission into the Pioneers' Home, but in July 1931 decided to appeal to a higher power when a favorable response was slow in coming. Governor Hunt and Kate had met in Globe where she ran a boarding house and saloon. A letter written to C. M. Zander, the secretary of the Board of Directors of State Institutions, explained how concerned she was with her poor circumstances in Dos Cabezas.[6]

"Dear Mr. Zander, no doubt you have received documents regard to my application for admittance to the pioneer home from Mr. C. O. Anderson my attorney.

"When may I leave Dos Cabezas for that home? I have money to pay my fare to Prescott, but when I arrive in the city I won't know where to go or what to do with myself. I would like to leave here soon as you have accommodations for me. I am very anxious to leave here [as] I have no income to pay my expenses here.

"If you write me when I can come please give me a few days to dispose of some furniture and a few other things; if I stay here much longer I won't have money enough left to pay my fare or anything else.

"Please let me here [sic] from you at your earliest convenience.

"I remain most respectfully, Mrs. Mary K. Cummings."[7]

Either Kate's appeal to Governor Hunt made an impression or space at the Pioneers' Home opened at the same time because a letter was sent to Kate on September 1, 1931.

"My Dear Mrs. Cummings," the letter from C. M. Zander began. "It is my pleasure to inform you that the Board of Directors has approved your admission to the Pioneers' Home and you may make arrangements to go to the Home immediately.

"Mr. Dan J. Seaman, Superintendent of the Home, has been notified of this action and this letter will serve as your introduction to him. This approval must be taken advantage of within thirty days.

"Very truly yours, Board of Directors of State Institutions."[8]

By the end of September 1931, Kate was living at the Pioneers' Home and getting to know the other residents and the daily routine. All seemed to be going well for a while. Political leaders and former members of the Board of Directors of State Institutions visited the facility and met with the people who lived there. At Christmastime, holiday parties were held for the residents, and according to the December 26, 1931, edition of the *Arizona Daily Star*, Santa Claus stopped by with presents for everyone. An anonymous donor got into the spirit, too, and gave each guest at the home five dollars to thank them for their part in helping to build the state.[9]

A few residents at the home had written memoirs about their adventures in Arizona's early days. William Shooter, a freight wagon driver in 1873, provided the Arizona Pioneers' Historical Society with his written tales about hauling supplies to mining camps from Hardyville to Prescott. George Bernard wrote of his time as a justice of the peace in Prescott in 1863, and Dr. John Charles Handy penned his autobiography about his years practicing medicine in Pima County. Kate believed she had a story to tell and hoped someone would come forward with a substantial amount of money to pay her to write it. Until that time, she spent her days resting, sewing, and reflecting upon her life.[10]

For a while, Kate was pleased with the care she received at the Arizona Pioneers' Home. The first indication Kate was dissatisfied with her living arrangement was in July 1934. She wrote a letter to Arthur N. Kelley, secretary of the Board of Directors of State Institutions with complaints about overcrowding and the home's superintendent.

"Dear Mr. Kelley, I am writing to see if you can give me any assistance. I know you have the power, if you so use it. I have been in the Home three years this September. I am 84 years old. [I] think I am too old to have so much disturbance. The Superintendent [sic] seems to delight in moving us from one room to another. Just when one gets good and settled and try [sic] to be happy she moves not only me but many more and we are certainly getting tired. I am in a small room with another lady now and we are so crowded I just cannot stand it. I am so upset all the time that I am on the verge of a breakdown. [The] lady I am with is very nice and we get along fine, only we are so crowded. We know of two or three rooms that are not in use. We also know she [the superintendent] is holding rooms for these nurses that live outside who have their own homes and those rooms are for lady guests into the Home. She has moved me three times and I haven't had any trouble with any of the ladies or the nurses, but it is rocky. I am asking you not to send this letter back to our superintendent, Mrs. Ryekman. If you do I know she will make it that much harder for me. I understand that you return all letters you get from the guests to Mrs. Ryekman.

"I could tell you many more things, but do not want to take so [much] of your time, but I will tell you this that we are all afraid of our shadows.

"You know that is not a very pleasant Home feeling. We are afraid to talk to each other. I hope you will do something for us.

"Thank you in advance. I am respectfully, Mrs. Mary K. Cummings."[11] On August 3, 1934, Arthur Kelley kindly responded to Kate's letter.

"My Dear Mrs. Cummings, receipt is acknowledged of your recent communications, and I have given the subject matter therein careful perusal.

"It is of course impossible for me, without knowing all the complications under which any superintendent of your Institution must necessarily be confronted, to know just what might be the advisable procedure. I can readily see the impossibility of any superintendent being able to operate the Pioneers' Home to the full satisfaction of all guests. It occurs to me, if there are rooms in the Institution not being used that would be more commodious than the one now occupied by you and one other lady, there must be some good reason, with which neither you nor myself are familiar. It is my belief that the large majority of guests appreciate the efforts being made by Mrs. Ryekman to keep the Home clean and give everyone there the very best possible within the range of the financial budget under which she is forced to operate. It should of course be the aim of any superintendent to do everything possible for the comfort, health and happiness of those people who find it a convenient haven in their old age. This however can be accomplished only with the full cooperation of the entire personnel, not only of the employees but the guests as well.

"There are many inconveniences one counters in the daily life of all of us, and if those of us are younger and still able to battle life attempt to compare our lots with those who are more fortunate, who live in larger houses and have more conveniences, we would be more or less unhappy. Contentment of mind lies within the individual.

"I cannot believe that Mrs. Ryekman or any other fair-minded person would deliverately [sic] attempt to make it inconvenient for anyone in the Home. There must be some other reason for moving the guests from one room to another as stated by you. Some of these reasons may be due to the dissatisfaction and complaints of some guests themselves, and in her endeavor to satisfy those complaints, she may naturally cause resentment in the minds of others.

"I will not indicate to Mrs. Ryekman that you have communicated with me and if the opportunity arises in the near future I will talk the matter over with her, and endeavor to find just what the difficulties may be, and it is just possible that steps can be taken to eliminate further dissatisfaction on the part of those who feel they could be made more contented.

"Won't you please assist in quelling any talk among the guests, which might spread and cause dissatisfaction even to some who are now fairly contented. It is my opinion that if every guest would give a little thought to the difficulties which any superintendent must encounter, and a slightly more charitable feeling existed, many of the apparent difficulties would vanish.

"Very sincerely yours, Board of Directors of State Institutions, Arthur N. Kelley, Secretary."[12]

Kate was not satisfied with Kelley's plan to resolve the issues she brought to his attention. On September 15, 1934, she penned a letter to Arizona governor Benjamin Baker Moeur.

"Dear Mr. Moeur, Sometime last month I appealed to Mr. Kelley, secretary of board of State institutions about conditions in Pioneers' Home. His answer insinuated that I ought to be glad to be in this Home on any condition. I am glad to be here, but not on these prison conditions. My roommate is a very nice lady to get along with, she has a few pieces of furniture, this room is very small. Everything she has is piled between her bed and the wall if she wants to get to her trunk she has to pull her furniture and climb over her bed. There isn't space enough in this room to give it any open cleaning. Neither or us is strong enough to move furniture to clean underneath. There was an open room, the Super could have let one of us move into, it was vacant over two months. The room is big enough for two beds, there is one bed in it.

"Yesterday she moved one of the ladies out of a nice little comfortable room into this bigger room, then she moved another lady into the small room. Neither of those ladies have any extra furniture only what the Home furnishes. The old lady she moved into the small room has a grandson. He is courting Mrs. Ryekman's niece, Miss Jean Fairbanks. She raises birds for all of them, that is why she is one of the favorites.

"I think this Home needs a man at the head of it. If any of the ladies become popular here she gets jealous and she will do any mean thing to annoy her. There would be more room for the ladies if their part wasn't taken up for hospital use too.

"I asked her one time for the vacant room. She said it was spoken for long ago. Another time that it was reserved for a married couple. The married couple never came, so put one of the old timers in. Our rations are most drastically cut. There is plenty put on the table, but it is not properly cooked. I don't blame the cooks. They have to do as she tells them or lose their job. You have no idea how much food goes off those tables into the swill barrel. She is starving us that way and that's called economy. She boasts on her saving fourteen thousand dollars for the State in her first year of service. The way she is doing now she will save twenty thousand dollars in this her second year.

"Here is a salad we get most every day; lettuce cut in big pieces with one or two tomatoes cut into four pieces. If we don't eat it, it goes into the swill barrel. Everything that she puts on the plate is frozen. We seldom get any fresh vegetables. Only canned carrots and peas. How would you like to live on such [a] delicate diet?

"My sight is very poor. I haven't had any eye drops for months. The nurse told me there wasn't any more, that it's very expensive. I am very old, will be eighty-four this coming November. I will be here three years the 27th of this month. I never had any trouble with the guests or any of the nurses or any hired help. There is not a nurse that can say anything against me.

"This Super is doing you more harm than good in this election. Should you be reelected, appoint a man that has dignity about him and kindness which [the] Super has not. She may make a good matron in a police station. She is no good here. She boasts of how she bailed one and or two out.

"I appeal to you Mr. Moeur, to help us out. If you are reelected, you can help by appointing a good man. She is sure you will reappoint her on her saving qualities.

"Most respectfully, Mrs. Mary K. Cummings."[13]

Governor Moeur forwarded Kate's letter to Secretary Kelley. By October 3, 1934, Kelley had sent Kate his response.

"My Dear Mrs. Cummings, Your communication of the 15th, which was turned to this office for reply, has not sooner been given consideration owing to the fact that I have been away from the office between the dates of September 15 and October 1.

"Please be assured we deeply regret that you are not satisfied with the accommodations being afforded by the Home. It has been the impression of the Governor and the other members of the Board, that the vast majority of guests felt everything possible was being done for their comfort without discrimination. The budget for the two-year period ending June 30, 1935, as allowed by the State Legislature is some $35,000,000 less than the budget for the two-year period ending June 30, 1933, which makes a saving necessary.

"On my next visit to the Home, I will be only too pleased to talk with you regarding the subject matter of your letter. In the meantime, we sincerely trust that some of the causes for dissatisfaction may have disappeared.

"It is assumed you still desire us not to indicate to the management that you have communicated with the office.

"Very respectfully yours, Board of Directors of State Institutions, Arthur N. Kelley, Secretary."[14]

Kate's letter eventually brought about the outcome she had hoped. Her letter to Kelley dated October 8, 1934, explained what had transpired since she last wrote him.

"Dear Mr. Kelley, Received your letter. Through your kind influence, Mrs. Ryekman has given me a nice little room. I thank you very much for your kindness to me.

"Dear Kelley, I cannot understand why you sent me a copy of the letter sent to you and one to his Excellency Governor B. B. Moeur. Mr. Kelley, please return my original letters and I will return your copies. Your copies do not conform with my letters.

"I too will be pleased to see you on your next visit to the Home, but I want our talk to be in the office and not in the lobby.

"Most respectfully yours, Mrs. Mary K. Cummings."[15]

In a letter dated October 11, 1934, Arthur Kelley informs Kate how pleased he is to hear from her again.

"My Dear Mrs. Cummings, Receipt is acknowledged of your letter of October 8. It is very gratifying indeed to know that certain changes made by Mrs. Ryekman have made conditions more satisfactory, and I sincerely trust you will have no further occasion for complaints. In all fairness to Mrs. Ryekman, however, I must state that the changes you mention were made on her own volition, as this office had not yet had the opportunity to contact her and was awaiting the time when another visit could be made to the Home, as we desired to follow your instructions regarding your request to keep your correspondence confidential.

"As your last communication was addressed to the Governor and turned to this office for reply, it was proper procedure to file your original letter here and forward to the governor's office [a] copy of your letter, together with copy of my reply, so that the files in his office would also show the transaction. A copy of your letter was returned to you, realizing that you probably had not kept a copy of this correspondence and that you might be interested in having it in your possession along with my reply. We have checked your original letter with the copy forwarded you and find it is an exact copy.

"I will be only too pleased to visit you when I find the opportunity to again be in Prescott, and in the mean time I sincerely trust you will be comfortable and that your health will remain good.

"Very truly yours, Arthur N. Kelley, Secretary."[16]

During Kate's stay at the Pioneers' Home, she was approached by more than one ambitious author hoping to persuade her to allow him to write a book about her life and times. She was not willing to embark on such a venture unless they were willing to pay her for her story. It appears none of those authors offered near the amount Kate believed her tale to be worth. She did speak to two men about her adventurous life. They were Anton Mazzanovich and Dr. Arthur Bork. Mazzanovich was a respected cavalry soldier and author who focused on writing about the West. His most popular work, entitled *Trailing Geronimo,* was released in 1931. Mazzanovich managed to get some information from Kate before she refused to share more until he paid her for her time. Dr. Bork, a graduate student at the University of Arizona, was asked by a friend of Kate's to visit with her in 1935. Bork, too, only got so far in his interviews with the strong-willed Kate before she stopped talking. She wanted money to continue.[17]

On November 2, 1940, just five days before she was to turn ninety years old, Mary K. Cummings, also known as Kate Elder, passed away. The cause of death was listed as acute myocardial insufficiency. Kate's funeral service was held on November 7, 1940, at the Ruffner Funeral Home in Prescott. Reverend Arthur S. Crook officiated the service. Kate had been an Arizonian for sixty-four years. She was survived by her sister

Mary K. Cummings's headstone
COURTESY OF SHARLOT HALL MUSEUM LIBRARY AND ARCHIVES C-130 ITEM 2

Mrs. Wilma Westchall of Buffalo, Iowa, and her niece Lillian Rafferty of Denver, Colorado.[18]

In a letter Kate wrote to her niece on March 18, 1940, she concluded her correspondence, where she shared highlights of her intrepid days, with the following sentiments: "Some is sad and some is quite laughable, but such is life anyway we take it."[19]

Kate was laid to rest at the Pioneers' Home Cemetery under a headstone reading simply: Mary K. Cummings 1850–1940. Her grave is regularly adorned with flowers.

Chapter Ten

The Legend of Kate Elder

THE OLD WEST LEGENDS OF KATE ELDER, MANY DISCREDITED BY CEN-turies of scrutiny, still strike a chord in America's hearts and minds. Kate herself was often shocked and dismayed by how legend portrayed her. Stuart Lake, who wrote the first biography about Wyatt Earp with Earp contributing to the work, referred to Kate as "Big-Nose Kate" and added that when she wasn't "writhing under Doc's [Holliday] scorn, she'd get drunk as well as furious and make Doc more trouble than any shooting scrape."[1] Kate was annoyed with the mischaracterization and resented Lake and Earp's portrayal of her. "Wyatt Earp had a deep-seated grudge against Mrs. Holliday," Kate's biographer Anton Mazzanovich wrote, "and he did his best to separate her from Doc."[2]

Wyatt Earp, obviously, didn't care for Kate, and the book *Wyatt Earp: Frontier Marshal* reflected his low opinion of her. His reason for describing her as he did was personal. The same could be said for journalist Joe Chisholm. Chisholm sought Kate out in the late 1930s in hopes of writing a book about her life. Kate refused to cooperate with Chisholm unless he paid her. In retaliation, he fabricated a story about Kate being shot up the rectum and killed while in Bisbee with Doc rushing to the scene too late to save her. Chisholm's take contends that Doc performed an examination on his paramour to learn exactly how she died. It was during his inspection that he finds she was shot and exactly where the bullet entered the body. The motivation behind the graphic and purely invented tale was to humiliate Kate.[3]

In addition to the fictionalized accounts of Kate's life and times written by Lake, Earp, and Chisholm, there were several newspaper articles and comic strips that portrayed her time west of Davenport, Iowa, with Doc Holliday as merely a carefree adventure. A story in the March 15, 1942, edition of the *San Francisco Examiner* depicts Kate as a gun-toting wild woman interested only in shooting up the town with Doc when citizens in various western locations tried to interfere with their good time. A *Lone Ranger* comic strip in the early 1950s portrayed Kate and Doc as crusaders against outlaws and warring tribes of Indians.[4]

Poems have been written about Kate's time with Doc, referring to their relationship as romantic and destructive. Songs celebrate Kate's spirit and curse her part in Doc's downfall. Saloons have been named after Kate as well as special beers and whiskey. The description on bottles of Big Nose Kate Sour notes that Kate's "fiery and flamboyant character was one to avoid on her whiskey days." The implication of course is that Kate was a hard drinker.[5]

Kate has been portrayed in a variety of radio programs, television shows, and motion pictures. Radio audiences in the 30s and 40s knew of Kate Elder through the broadcasts *Frontier Gentleman*, *Frontier Town*, and *The Six Shooter*. Television viewers learned about Kate when they tuned into the popular shows *Gunsmoke* and *The Legend of Wyatt Earp*. On the small screen, Kate was portrayed by actresses Carol Montgomery Stone, Collette Lyons, and Peggy Knudsen. In motion pictures, Kate Elder was portrayed by Linda Darnell, Jo Van Fleet, Faye Dunaway, and Joanna Pacula. In director John Ford's film *My Darling Clementine*, Doc Holliday's paramour was named Chihuahua. The saloon girl, the only similarity to Doc's real-life love interest, is shot in the film, and Doc operates on her to remove the bullet. A review in the December 14, 1946, edition of the *Los Angeles Times* praises Ford's "keen and sensitive directing eye," but notes the history is grossly inaccurate. Linda Darnell's performance was singled out as being her "finest to date."[6]

Actress Jo Van Fleet's portrayal of Big-Nose Kate in *Gunfight at the O.K. Corral* is truer to Kate's character. Kirk Douglas plays Doc Holliday in the film, and the combative relationship Van Fleet and Douglas act out on camera mirrors the difficulties Kate and Doc had at times in real life. Douglas did his own knife throwing in the film, and Van Fleet, in the interest of realism, refused a double and acted as his target for a scene in

Linda Darnell sits between Henry Fonda and Victor Mature; the three starred together in *My Darling Clementine*. PAUL HUTTON COLLECTION

Jo Van Fleet stands between Kirk Douglas and John Ireland in the film *Gunfight at the O.K. Corral*. PAUL HUTTON COLLECTION

which he vents his ill temper by tracing her silhouette with knives against a wooden door.[7]

Powder River, released in June 1953, was another film based on the book *Wyatt Earp: Frontier Marshal*. In this version, the characters' names were changed, and a few scenes from the original text were omitted. Rory Calhoun played a Wyatt Earp–like marshal, and Cameron Mitchell played a Doc Holliday–type sidekick. Corinne Calvet took on the role of Frenchie Dumont, a saloon owner romantically involved with Mitchell's character. A review in an edition of the *Shamokin News-Dispatch* called *Powder River* a "roaring technicolor drama which underscores the westward flow of rugged pioneer ancestors." The article called Calvet's Big-Nose Kate–type character "shrewd, beautiful and calculating."[8]

In the film *Doc*, released in August 1971, Kate is played by Faye Dunaway and Doc Holliday by Stacy Keach. Doc wins Kate in a poker game, and he gives her a ride to Tombstone on the rear of his horse. In Tombstone, she finds employment in a brothel. A review of Dunaway's portrayal of Kate Elder in the August 5, 1971, edition of the *Boston Globe* noted she had "moments of actress conviction, although she was never really believable, in fact, she is very close to ridiculous."[9]

Polish actress Joanna Pacula's total screen time as Kate Elder in the 1993 film *Tombstone* was less than ten minutes. Critics noted her portrayal was "effective but brief."[10]

In the summer of 1994, the film *Wyatt Earp* opened in theaters across the country. Kevin Costner starred as Wyatt Earp, Dennis Quaid as Doc Holliday, and Isabella Rossellini as Big-Nose Kate. Film critic Roger Ebert called *Wyatt Earp* a "rambling, unfocused biography."[11]

The 1965 movie *The Sons of Katie Elder*, starring John Wayne and Dean Martin, didn't feature Kate Elder at all. Based on a story by Academy

Faye Dunaway and Stacey Keach portrayed Kate Elder and Doc Holliday in the 1971 feature *Doc*. PAUL HUTTON COLLECTION

Award–winning writer Talbot Jennings, the four Elder brothers return to the town where their mother, Katie, lived to attend her funeral. According to Jennings, the name Katie Elder was inspired by the real-life Kate Elder.[12]

The only motion picture Kate was personally familiar with was *Frontier Marshal* which premiered in July 1939. Based on the book of the same title Stuart Lake wrote with Wyatt Earp contributing, *Frontier Marshal* starred Randolph Scott as Wyatt Earp and Cesar Romero as Doc Holliday. Binnie Barnes portrayed the character Jerry, based loosely on Kate Elder. The August 12, 1939, edition of *The Gazette* called the picture a "triumph." Randolph Scott's and Cesar Romero's acting was lauded and the story praised for being "sharp-shooting."[13]

"When *Frontier Marshal* gets going it centers around the two saloons opposing Wyatt Earp with a mess of gamblers and bandits," the review explained. "Chief among these is Doc Halliday [sic], driven out West from a medical practice in Illinois to become a dangerous man. Good and bad angels to Halliday are two women, one a dance hall blonde, the other the girl who has followed him from back East. The conflict between the two women, while not especially subtle, provides many of the best moments."[14]

Kate read many of the articles printed about the book and movie *Frontier Marshal*, and the more she read the more furious she became. She resented that Doc was portrayed as a "frequent drinker and gunslinger." Kate insisted he wasn't a person to instigate a fight or that he indulged as often as the book and film led people to believe. She also took exception with the type of woman Doc was supposed to have been involved. It was Kate's frustration with *Frontier Marshal*, both the book and the film, that led her to agree to meet with writers hoping to pen her biography.[15]

Two years after Kate passed away, the *San Francisco Examiner* ran a five-page article about the event at the O.K. Corral. Kate's tempestuous relationship with Doc was covered in the report. More than fifty years had passed since the gunfight in Tombstone occurred, and readers still had an appetite for the legendary tale. Kate's death brought a resurgence of interest in the rowdy days of the Old West. Newspaper reports about her time with Doc Holliday and where she had spent her last days surfaced.

Binnie Barnes (right) starred as a Kate Elder–type in the film *Frontier Marshal*; Cesar Romero portrayed Doc Holliday. PAUL HUTTON COLLECTION

Some articles described her life and times as "one lacking in morals or integrity."[16] Others made sport of her physical appearance, claiming she was "in every way unattractive." A column in the April 20, 1946, edition of the *Shamokin News-Dispatch* entitled "Voices of Broadway" made the following comment about her looks. "I doubt if any casting director in his right mind would okay any of the glamour girls of that day [the 1800s], with the possible exceptions of Belle Starr and Dora Hand, who were both beauties. Kitty the Schemer, Poker Alice, Big-Nose Kate (she and Doc Holliday were a heart toddy), Mme Moustache, Cattle Kate and Calamity Jane, if their names are any indication, would give Boris Karloff the screaming memies."[17]

According to some magazine articles, Kate Elder was from Illinois, possessed a large nose, and operated a brothel in Tombstone. Other publications insisted she was born into an aristocratic family and that she was strictly a singer and dancer in saloons across the West. At some point, the truth about Kate and where she came from was lost to folklore.

When Kate refused to tell the whole story of her life and times, she left much to speculation and conjecture. For those historians, filmmakers, writers, and poets who desire her story be recorded for posterity's sake, they mostly have only the legend to draw from—and that's a fact.

Endnotes

Chapter One The Girl from Hungary

1 Professor A. W. Bork Notes/Letters/Interview with Kate Elder, Kate's family and friends compiled 1935-1978.

2 Ibid.

3 Ibid.

4 Kate Elder's handwritten notes about her life including her time as Mrs. John Henry Holliday written 1935-1939.

5 *Dodge City: Cowboy Capital*, 12-15; *Dodge City: Up through a Century in Story and Pictures*, 34-37.

6 Kate Elder's handwritten notes about her life including her time as Mrs. John Henry Holliday written 1935-1939.

7 www.worldportsource.com Port of Bremen, Germany.

8 Kate Elder's handwritten notes about her life including her time as Mrs. John Henry Holliday written 1935-1939, www.ancestry.com Mary Katherine Horony.

9 *Passenger List of Vessels arriving at New York, 1820–1897*. Microfilm Publication M237, Roll 205, List 901, Steamship *Bremen*, September 19, 1860, pp. 6–7. NAT: 6256867. Records of the US Customs Service, Record Group 36. National Archives at Washington, DC.

10 www.worldportsource.com

11 *Davenport Daily Gazette*, April 29, 1865, Naturalization Index Scott County, Iowa, 1842-1930.

12 Kate Elder's handwritten notes about her life including her time as Mrs. John Henry Holliday written 1935-1939; www.ancestry.com Mary Katherine Horony.

13 *Davenport Daily Gazette*, April 29, 1865

14 Kate Elder's handwritten notes about her life including her time as Mrs. John Henry Holliday written 1935-1939; www.ancestry.com Mary Katherine Horony; www.ancestry.com Iowa, Wills and Probate Records, 1758-1997.

15 Kate Elder's handwritten notes about her life including her time as Mrs. John Henry Holliday written 1935-1939, Scott County Court, Reel #101 1865 Report of Otto Smith, re: Harony minors and probate record.

16 Email exchange between Chris Enss and Sr. Thomas More Daley, OSU Archivist, Ursuline Archives, Central Province, USA, emails dated December 20, 2017, January 17, 2019, February 27, 2018, and February 28, 2018; *Lincoln County Herald*, June 1, 1856.

17 Email exchange between Chris Enss and Sr. Thomas More Daley, OSU Archivist, Ursuline Archives, Central Province, USA, emails dated December 20, 2017, January 17, 2019, February 27, 2018, and February 28, 2018; *Saint Louis: The Future Great City of the World*, 74-75.

18 Kate Elder's handwritten notes about her life including her time as Mrs. John Henry Holliday written 1935-1939.

19 Prologue: *Quarterly of National Archives*. "Bridging the Mississippi: The Railroads and Steamboats Clash at the Rock Island Bridge," David A. Pfeiffer.

20 www.slate.com/blogs/thevault.

21 Kate Elder's handwritten notes about her life including her time as Mrs. John Henry Holliday written 1935-1939.

22 Kate Elder's handwritten notes about her life including her time as Mrs. John Henry Holliday written 1935-1939; Kate Elder's letters to her niece Lillian Lane Rafferty written between May 1935 and March 1940.

23 *Rochester Daily Union*, October 10, 1866.

24 Kate Elder's handwritten notes about her life including her time as Mrs. John Henry Holliday written 1935-1939; Kate Elder's letters to her niece Lillian Lane Rafferty written between May 1935 and March 1940.

25 Kate Elder's letters to her niece Lillian Lane Rafferty written between May 1935 and March 1940; *Tri-Weekly Examiner*, August 6, 1869.

26 Kate Elder's letters to her niece Lillian Lane Rafferty written between May 1935 and March 1940.

27 www.ancestry.com Iowa, Wills and Probate Records, 1758-1997.

28 https://stlouis-mo.gov/government/department.

29 *Saint Louis: The Future Great City of the World*, 82-88; https://stlouis-mo.gov/government/department; Kate Elder's handwritten notes about her life including her time as Mrs. John Henry Holliday written 1935-1939.

30 Kate Elder's handwritten notes about her life including her time as Mrs. John Henry Holliday written 1935-1939; Professor A. W. Bork Notes/Letters/Interview with Kate Elder, Kate's family and friends compiled 1935-1978; http://genealogy.mohistory.org/geneaology/name/161167?a=1.

31 Professor A. W. Bork Notes/Letters/Interview with Kate Elder, Kate's family and friends compiled 1935-1978.

32 Ibid.

33 *Chicago Tribune*, July 31, 1870; *Leavenworth Weekly*, November 24, 1870; *Detroit Free Press*, July 14, 1870.

34 US Census, 1870.

35 *Renegade History of the United States*, 102-104.

36 Professor A. W. Bork Notes/Letters/Interview with Kate Elder, Kate's family and friends compiled 1935-1978; *Renegade History of the United States*, 102-104.

37 *Renegade History of the United States*, 102-104.

38 Ibid.

39 Professor A. W. Bork Notes/Letters/Interview with Kate Elder, Kate's family and friends compiled 1935-1978; Kate Elder's handwritten notes about her life including her time as Mrs. John Henry Holliday written 1935-1939.

Chapter Two Soiled Dove in a Cow Town
1 *Weekly Caucasian*, January 27, 1872.

2 Ibid.

3 Kate Elder's handwritten notes about her life including her time as Mrs. John Henry Holliday written 1935-1939; Professor A. W. Bork Notes/Letters/Interview with Kate Elder, Kate's family and friends compiled 1935-1978.

4 *Weekly Caucasian*, January 27, 1872; *St. Louis Post Dispatch*, March 3, 1874.

5 *Kansas History Journal*, vol. 2, no. 1, spring 1979.

6 *Macon Republican*, August 29, 1872.

7 Ibid.

8 *St. Louis Weekly Democrat*, February 6, 1872.

9 Missouri Census Records, 1865-1895.

10 *New York Tribune*, March 21, 1872.

11 *Brothels, Bordellos, and Bad Girls: Prostitution in Colorado* 1860-1930, 1-5.

12 Author Anton Mazzanovich Notes/Interview with Kate Elder June 1932–November 1932.

13 *Doc Holliday: A Family Portrait*, 9-11; *Doc Holliday: The Life and Legend*, 16-19.

14 Author Anton Mazzanovich Notes/Interview with Kate Elder June 1932–November 1932.

15 *Doc Holliday: The Life and Legend*, 58-59.

16 Author Anton Mazzanovich Notes/Interview with Kate Elder June 1932–November 1932.

17 Ibid.

18 *Doc Holliday: The Life and Legend*, 10-16.

19 *Doc Holliday: The Life and Legend*, 59-62; *Doc Holliday: A Family Portrait*, 77-80.

20 https://history-ray's place.com/ks/se-wichita-early.htm.

21 Ibid.

22 *Wichita Daily Eagle*, August 10, 1871; *Kansas History Journal*, vol. 2, spring 1977.

23 *Kansas History Journal*, vol. 2, spring 1977; *I Married Wyatt Earp*, 56-57.

24 Wichita City Records Misc. Papers 1874; *Kansas History Journal*, vol. 2, spring 1977; Arrest/Court Records Bessie Earp and Sallie Earp, September 15, 1874.

25 *Wichita Eagle*, May 28, 1873.

26 *Kansas History Journal*, vol. 2, spring 1977; *Wild West Magazine*, vol. 29, no. 3, October 2016.

27 Arrest/Court Records Bessie Earp and Sallie Earp, September 15, 1874.

28 *Wichita Weekly Eagle*, June 21, 1873, July 19, 1873, August 2, 1874.

29 Wichita City Records Misc. Papers 1874.

30 Ibid.

31 *Wichita Weekly Eagle*, January 8, 1874.

32 Professor A. W. Bork Notes/Letters/Interview with Kate Elder, Kate's family and friends compiled 1935-1978.

33 *Great Bend Register*, July 9, 1874.

34 Kate Elder's handwritten notes about her life including her time as Mrs. John Henry Holliday written 1935-1939.

35 *Great Bend Register*, August 20, 1874.

36 *Dodge City: Up through a Century in Story and Pictures*, 18-21.

37 Ford County Historical Society research paper, " Girls of the Golden West"; Kate Elder's handwritten notes about her life including her time as Mrs. John Henry Holliday written 1935-1939.
38 *Atchison Daily Champion*, August 7, 1875.
39 Kansas Census Records, 1864-1885.
40 Ford County Historical Society research paper, "Girls of the Golden West"; Kate Elder's handwritten notes about her life including her time as Mrs. John Henry Holliday written 1935-1939.
41 *Weekly Atchison Champion*, August 14, 1875.
42 Kate Elder's handwritten notes about her life including her time as Mrs. John Henry Holliday written 1935-1939; Professor A. W. Bork Notes/Letters/Interview with Kate Elder, Kate's family and friends compiled 1935-1978.
43 *Weekly Commonwealth*, September 9, 1875.
44 *Chase County Leader*, July 10, 1875.
45 Kate Elder's handwritten notes about her life including her time as Mrs. John Henry Holliday written 1935-1939; Professor A. W. Bork Notes/Letters/Interview with Kate Elder, Kate's family and friends compiled 1935-1978; Ford County Historical Society research paper, "Girls of the Golden West"; *Dodge City Times*, March 9, 1879.
46 Ford County Historical Society research paper, "Girls of the Golden West."
47 *Atchison Daily Champion*, April 9, 1875.
48 *Leavenworth Times*, October 31, 1875; *Atchison Daily Champion*, August 22, 1875.
49 *Wichita Daily Eagle*, July 15, 1874.
50 Kate Elder's handwritten notes about her life including her time as Mrs. John Henry Holliday written 1935-1939; Professor A. W. Bork Notes/Letters/Interview with Kate Elder, Kate's family and friends compiled 1935-1978.
51 Ibid.

Chapter Three Riding with Doc Holliday
1 Ibid.
2 https://tshaonline.org/handbook/online/articles/hlm77 Mobeetie, Texas.
3 Kate Elder's handwritten notes about her life including her time as Mrs. John Henry Holliday written 1935-1939.
4 *Osage County Chronicle*, August 24, 1876.
5 *Famous Gunfighters of the Western Frontier*, 5-6; *Doc Holliday: A Family Portrait*, 123-126.
6 *Doc Holliday: A Family Portrait*, 123-126; *Daily Commonwealth*, February 26, 1876.
7 *Daily Commonwealth*, February 26, 1876.
8 *Hell's Half Acre*, 110-112.
9 *Hell's Half Acre*, 110-112; https://www.texasbeyondhistory.net/forts/griffin/index.html.
10 *Hell's Half Acre*, 110-112.
11 Kate Elder's handwritten notes about her life including her time as Mrs. John Henry Holliday written 1935-1939; *Brothels, Bordellos, and Bad Girls: Prostitution in Colorado 1860-1930*, 55-58.

12 *Austin American-Statesman*, January 31, 1963, *Wicked Women: Notorious, Mischievous, and Wayward Ladies from the Old West*, 25-32

13 The Austin American-Statesman, January 31, 1963; *Wicked Women: Notorious, Mischievous, and Wayward Ladies from the Old West*, 25-32.

14 *Doc Holliday: A Family Portrait*, 112-115.

15 Kate Elder's handwritten notes about her life including her time as Mrs. John Henry Holliday written 1935-1939; Professor A. W. Bork Notes/Letters/Interview with Kate Elder, Kate's family and friends compiled 1935-1978; author Anton Mazzanovich Notes/Interview with Kate Elder June 1932–November 1932; *Street Fight in Tombstone, Near the OK*, 75-76.

16 Kate Elder's handwritten notes about her life including her time as Mrs. John Henry Holliday written 1935-1939; Professor A. W. Bork Notes/Letters/Interview with Kate Elder, Kate's family and friends compiled 1935-1978; *Wyatt Earp: The Life behind the Legend*, 17-18; Tombstone, 49-50.

17 Kate Elder's handwritten notes about her life including her time as Mrs. John Henry Holliday written 1935-1939; Professor A. W. Bork Notes/Letters/Interview with Kate Elder, Kate's family and friends compiled 1935-1978; author Anton Mazzanovich Notes/Interview with Kate Elder June 1932–November 1932.

18 Kate Elder's handwritten notes about her life including her time as Mrs. John Henry Holliday written 1935-1939; Professor A. W. Bork Notes/Letters/Interview with Kate Elder, Kate's family and friends compiled 1935-1978; author Anton Mazzanovich Notes/Interview with Kate Elder June 1932–November 1932.

19 *San Francisco Examiner*, August 2, 1896.

20 Author Anton Mazzanovich Notes/Interview with Kate Elder June 1932–November 1932.

21 *Doc Holliday: A Family Portrait*, 113-115; *Doc Holliday: The Life and Legend*, 87-88; *Doctors of Another Calling: Physicians Who Are Known Best in Fields Other than Medicine*, 185-187.

22 Author Anton Mazzanovich Notes/Interview with Kate Elder June 1932–November 1932.

23 https://tshaonline.org/handbook/online/articles/exj01.

24 Ibid.

25 *Voyage to the United States*, vol. 3, chapter XXIV, "From San Antonio to Eagle Pass."

26 *Evening Star*, February 9, 1878.

27 Author Anton Mazzanovich Notes/Interview with Kate Elder June 1932–November 1932; Kate Elder's handwritten notes about her life including her time as Mrs. John Henry Holliday written 1935-1939; Professor A. W. Bork Notes/Letters/Interview with Kate Elder, Kate's family and friends compiled 1935-1978.

28 Ibid.

29 *Galveston Daily News*, May 21, 1878.

30 *Marshall Messenger*, January 10, 1879.

31 *Marshall Messenger*, January 10, 1879; *Tri-Weekly Herald*, May 13, 1878; *Galveston Daily News*, August 23, 1878.

32 *Dallas Daily Herald*, April 11, 1878.

33 *Austin American-Statesman*, February 21, 1877.

34 Author Anton Mazzanovich Notes/Interview with Kate Elder June 1932–November 1932; Kate Elder's handwritten notes about her life including her time as Mrs. John Henry Holliday written 1935-1939; Professor A. W. Bork Notes/Letters/Interview with Kate Elder, Kate's family and friends compiled 1935-1978.

35 *Tri-Weekly Herald*, October 19, 1878.

36 *The Black Regulars, 1866-1898*, 167-169.

37 Kate Elder's handwritten notes about her life including her time as Mrs. John Henry Holliday written 1935-1939.

38 *Tri-Weekly Herald*, October 15, 1878.

39 *Famous Gunfighters of the Western Frontier*, 38-39.

40 Kate Elder's handwritten notes about her life including her time as Mrs. John Henry Holliday written 1935-1939.

Chapter Four Time in Dodge City

1 *Winfield Courier*, May 30, 1878; Kate Elder's handwritten notes about her life including her time as Mrs. John Henry Holliday written 1935-1939.

2 Kate Elder's handwritten notes about her life including her time as Mrs. John Henry Holliday written 1935-1939.

3 Ibid.

4 Ibid.

5 *Dodge City Times*, June 27, 1878.

6 Ibid.

7 Dodge City Ordinances, No. 41 & No. 42, Dodge City Manual – 1878.

8 *Dodge City Times*, August 10, 1878.

9 *Dodge City Times*, August 17, 1878.

10 *Dodge City Times*, August 13, 1878.

11 *Dodge City Times*, August 20, 1878; *Dodge City Globe*, May 29, 1878.

12 Kate Elder's handwritten notes about her life including her time as Mrs. John Henry Holliday written 1935-1939; *Dodge City Times*, July 27, 1878; *Doc Holliday: A Family Portrait*, 123-124; *The Old West in Fact in Film: History Versus Hollywood*, 38-39.

13 Kate Elder's handwritten notes about her life including her time as Mrs. John Henry Holliday written 1935-1939; *Dodge City: Up through a Century in Story and Pictures*, 80-81.

14 Kate Elder's handwritten notes about her life including her time as Mrs. John Henry Holliday written 1935-1939; author Anton Mazzanovich Notes/Interview with Kate Elder June 1932–November 1932; Professor A. W. Bork Notes/Letters/Interview with Kate Elder, Kate's family and friends compiled 1935-1978.

15 Kate Elder's handwritten notes about her life including her time as Mrs. John Henry Holliday written 1935-1939; *Thunder over the Prairie: The True Story of a Murder and a Manhunt by the Greatest Posse of all Time*, 10-12.

16 *Globe Republican*, August 20, 1878; Kate Elder's handwritten notes about her life including her time as Mrs. John Henry Holliday written 1935-1939; *Thunder over the Prairie: The True Story of a Murder and a Manhunt by the Greatest Posse of all Time* 10-12.

17 *Globe Republican*, August 20, 1878.

18 *Doc Holliday: The Life and Legend*, 99-101.

19 *Globe Republican*, August 20, 1878.

20 Kate Elder's handwritten notes about her life including her time as Mrs. John Henry Holliday written 1935-1939; author Anton Mazzanovich Notes/Interview with Kate Elder June 1932–November 1932.

21 *Wyatt Earp: Frontier Marshal*, 197-198; Kate Elder's handwritten notes about her life including her time as Mrs. John Henry Holliday written 1935-1939.

22 *The Frontier World of Doc Holliday*, 125-126.

23 Kate Elder's handwritten notes about her life including her time as Mrs. John Henry Holliday written 1935-1939; *Love Untamed: Romances of the Old West*, 83-84.

24 152 Kate Elder's handwritten notes about her life including her time as Mrs. John Henry Holliday written 1935-1939.

25 153 Kate Elder's handwritten notes about her life including her time as Mrs. John Henry Holliday written 1935-1939; www.smithsonianmag.com/science-nature/how-tuberculosis-shaped-victorian-fashion-180959029.

26 Kate Elder's handwritten notes about her life including her time as Mrs. John Henry Holliday written 1935-1939; *Winchester Argus*, May 2, 1878.

27 Kate Elder's handwritten notes about her life including her time as Mrs. John Henry Holliday written 1935-1939.

28 *Dodge City Times*, December 14, 1878.

29 *Doc Holliday: The Life and Legend*, 101-102.

30 Kate Elder's handwritten notes about her life including her time as Mrs. John Henry Holliday written 1935-1939.

31 Kate Elder's handwritten notes about her life including her time as Mrs. John Henry Holliday written 1935-1939; www.smithsonianmag.com/science-nature/how-tuberculosis-shaped-victorian-fashion-180959029.

32 Ibid.

33 Kate Elder's handwritten notes about her life including her time as Mrs. John Henry Holliday written 1935-1939; author Anton Mazzanovich Notes/Interview with Kate Elder June 1932–November 1932.

34 *Taloga Star*, May 25, 1888.

35 Kate Elder's handwritten notes about her life including her time as Mrs. John Henry Holliday written 1935-1939; *Daily Republican*, August 16, 1935.

36 *Daily Republican*, August 16, 1935; Kate Elder's handwritten notes about her life including her time as Mrs. John Henry Holliday written 1935-1939.

37 Kate Elder's handwritten notes about her life including her time as Mrs. John Henry Holliday written 1935-1939; *Famous Gunfighters of the Western Frontier*, 40-41.

38 *Doc Holliday: A Family Portrait*, 126-127; Kate Elder's letters to her niece Lillian Lane Rafferty written between May 1935 and March 1940.

Chapter Five Leaving Las Vegas

1 Kate Elder's handwritten notes about her life including her time as Mrs. John Henry Holliday written 1935-1939; *Doc Holliday: A Family Portrait*, 126-127; https://www.sciencedirect.com/science/article/pii/S095461110600401X.

2 *Daily Gazette*, September 30, 1878.

3 Kate Elder's handwritten notes about her life including her time as Mrs. John Henry Holliday written 1935-1939.

4 https://www.legendsofamerica.com/nm-lasvegas, https://mainstreetlvnm.org/home/history-of-las-vegas.

5 Ibid.

6 Kate Elder's handwritten notes about her life including her time as Mrs. John Henry Holliday written 1935-1939; author Anton Mazzanovich Notes/Interview with Kate Elder June 1932–November 1932; Professor A. W. Bork Notes/Letters/Interview with Kate Elder, Kate's family and friends compiled 1935-1978; *The Wildest of the West*, 87-88.

7 *Las Vegas Gazette*, March 23, 1879.

8 *Las Vegas Gazette*, April 14, 1879.

9 *Las Vegas Daily Optic*, December 16, 1898; *Las Vegas Gazette*, September 14, 1879.

10 *Weekly New Mexican*, January 11, 1879.

11 "Authentic Life Story Doc Holliday: The West's Greatest Gunman," 15-16; San Miguel County, New Mexico Territory Criminal Record Book, 1876-1879, 391, 401-402.

12 San Miguel County, New Mexico Deed of Records, 1875-1885.

13 San Miguel County, New Mexico Territory Criminal Record Book, 1876-1879, 391, 401-402; *Doc Holliday: The Life and Legend*, 103-104; *Doc Holliday: A Family Portrait*, 128-129.

14 *Bat Masterson: The Man and the Legend*, 148-151.

15 *Las Vegas Optic*, July 20, 1881.

16 Kate Elder's handwritten notes about her life including her time as Mrs. John Henry Holliday written 1935-1939; author Anton Mazzanovich Notes/Interview with Kate Elder June 1932–November 1932; Professor A. W. Bork Notes/Letters/Interview with Kate Elder, Kate's family and friends compiled 1935-1978.

17 *Las Vegas Gazette*, July 29, 1879.

18 Ibid.

19 Ibid.

20 *Las Vegas Gazette*, July 29, 1879; *Cultural Intersections and Historic Preservation: A Study of Las Vegas, New Mexico*, 67-68.

21 *Famous Gunfighters of the Western Frontier*, 40-41.

22 Kate Elder's handwritten notes about her life including her time as Mrs. John Henry Holliday written 1935-1939; author Anton Mazzanovich Notes/Interview with Kate Elder June 1932–November 1932; Professor A. W. Bork Notes/Letters/Interview with Kate Elder, Kate's family and friends compiled 1935-1978; San Miguel County, New Mexico Territory Criminal Record Book, 1876-1879, 391, 401-402.

23 Author Anton Mazzanovich Notes/Interview with Kate Elder June 1932–November 1932.

24 *Wyatt Earp: The Life behind the Legend*, 36-37.

25 Kate Elder's handwritten notes about her life including her time as Mrs. John Henry Holliday written 1935-1939; author Anton Mazzanovich Notes/Interview with Kate Elder June 1932–November 1932; Professor A. W. Bork Notes/Letters/Interview with Kate Elder, Kate's family and friends compiled 1935-1978.

26 Author Anton Mazzanovich Notes/Interview with Kate Elder June 1932–November 1932.

27 Kate Elder's handwritten notes about her life including her time as Mrs. John Henry Holliday written 1935-1939; author Anton Mazzanovich Notes/Interview with Kate Elder June 1932–November 1932.

28 Kate Elder's handwritten notes about her life including her time as Mrs. John Henry Holliday written 1935-1939.

29 Kate Elder's handwritten notes about her life including her time as Mrs. John Henry Holliday written 1935-1939; Author Anton Mazzanovich Notes/Interview with Kate Elder June 1932–November 1932.

30 *Weekly Arizona Miner*, April 2, 1880.

31 Kate Elder's handwritten notes about her life including her time as Mrs. John Henry Holliday written 1935-1939; author Anton Mazzanovich Notes/Interview with Kate Elder June 1932–November 1932; Professor A. W. Bork Notes/Letters/Interview with Kate Elder, Kate's family and friends compiled 1935-1978.

32 Ibid.

33 Kate Elder's handwritten notes about her life including her time as Mrs. John Henry Holliday written 1935-1939; Kate Elder's letters to her niece Lillian Lane Rafferty written between May 1935 and March 1940.

34 Kate Elder's handwritten notes about her life including her time as Mrs. John Henry Holliday written 1935-1939; author Anton Mazzanovich Notes/Interview with Kate Elder June 1932–November 1932; Professor A. W. Bork Notes/Letters/Interview with Kate Elder, Kate's family and friends compiled 1935-1978.

Chapter Six Street Fight in Tombstone

1 Kate Elder's handwritten notes about her life including her time as Mrs. John Henry Holliday written 1935-1939.

2 *Arizona Weekly Citizen*, March 17, 1881.

3 Ibid.

4 Kate Elder's handwritten notes about her life including her time as Mrs. John Henry Holliday written 1935-1939; author Anton Mazzanovich Notes/Interview with Kate Elder June 1932–November 1932.

5 Kate Elder's handwritten notes about her life including her time as Mrs. John Henry Holliday written 1935-1939; *Doc Holliday: A Family Portrait*, 141-145, 150-153.

6 Ibid.

7 Ibid.

8 *Arizona Weekly Citizen*, March 24, 1881.

9 Kate Elder's handwritten notes about her life including her time as Mrs. John Henry Holliday written 1935-1939; author Anton Mazzanovich Notes/Interview with Kate Elder June 1932–November 1932.

10 Kate Elder's handwritten notes about her life including her time as Mrs. John Henry Holliday written 1935-1939; author Anton Mazzanovich Notes/Interview with Kate Elder June 1932–November 1932; *Arizona Weekly Star*, March 31, 1881; Cochise County the Territory of Arizona vs. John H. Holliday Criminal Register of Actions, Case #23.

11 Cochise County the Territory of Arizona vs. John H. Holliday Criminal Register of Actions, Case #30.

12 Kate Elder's handwritten notes about her life including her time as Mrs. John Henry Holliday written 1935-1939; author Anton Mazzanovich Notes/Interview with Kate Elder June 1932–November 1932; Professor A. W. Bork Notes/Letters/Interview with Kate Elder, Kate's family and friends compiled 1935-1978.

13 Ibid.

14 Ibid.

15 *When All Roads Led to Tombstone*, 8-11; Kate Elder's handwritten notes about her life including her time as Mrs. John Henry Holliday written 1935-1939; author Anton Mazzanovich Notes/Interview with Kate Elder June 1932–November 1932.

16 Ibid.

17 Kate Elder's handwritten notes about her life including her time as Mrs. John Henry Holliday written 1935-1939; author Anton Mazzanovich Notes/Interview with Kate Elder June 1932–November 1932.

18 Ibid.

19 Kate Elder's handwritten notes about her life including her time as Mrs. John Henry Holliday written 1935-1939.

20 Kate Elder's handwritten notes about her life including her time as Mrs. John Henry Holliday written 1935-1939; Doc *Holliday: A Family Portrait*, 153-154.

21 Ibid.

22 *Arizona Weekly Citizen*, August 28, 1881.

23 Ibid.

24 Kate Elder's handwritten notes about her life including her time as Mrs. John Henry Holliday written 1935-1939; Author Anton Mazzanovich Notes/Interview with Kate Elder June 1932–November 1932; *Arizona Weekly Citizen*, August 28, 1881.

25 Kate Elder's handwritten notes about her life including her time as Mrs. John Henry Holliday written 1935-1939; author Anton Mazzanovich Notes/Interview with Kate Elder June 193 –November 1932.

26 Ibid.

27 Kate Elder's handwritten notes about her life including her time as Mrs. John Henry Holliday written 1935-1939; author Anton Mazzanovich Notes/Interview with Kate Elder June 1932–November 1932; Professor A. W. Bork Notes/Letters/Interview with Kate Elder, Kate's family and friends compiled 1935-1978.

28 O.K. Corral Inquest, November 1881; Kate Elder's handwritten notes about her life including her time as Mrs. John Henry Holliday written 1935-1939; author Anton Mazzanovich Notes/Interview with Kate Elder June 1932–November 1932.

29 Kate Elder's handwritten notes about her life including her time as Mrs. John Henry Holliday written 1935-1939; author Anton Mazzanovich Notes/Interview with Kate Elder June 1932–November 1932.

30 *Arizona Weekly Citizen*, November 13, 1881.

31 Kate Elder's handwritten notes about her life including her time as Mrs. John Henry Holliday written 1935-1939.

32 Ibid.

33 Ibid.
34 Ibid.

Chapter Seven Mrs. George Cummings

1 https://www.miningfoundationsw.org/resources/documents/publications/history The Old Dominion Copper Mine by Wilbur A. Haak; Kate Elder's handwritten notes about her life including her time as Mrs. John Henry Holliday written 1935-1939.

2 Kate Elder's handwritten notes about her life including her time as Mrs. John Henry Holliday written 1935-1939.

3 Ibid.

4 Ibid.

5 https://www.miningfoundationsw.org/resources/documents/publications/history The Old Dominion Copper Mine by Wilbur A. Haak; *Globe, Arizona: The Life and Times of a Western Mining Town, 1864-1917*, 112-114.

6 O.K. Corral Inquest, November 1881.

7 Author Anton Mazzanovich Notes/Interview with Kate Elder June 1932–November 1932; Kate Elder's handwritten notes about her life including her time as Mrs. John Henry Holliday written 1935-1939; Professor A. W. Bork Notes/Letters/Interview with Kate Elder, Kate's family and friends compiled 1935-1978; *Tucson Citizen*, March 21, 1882; *Tombstone Epitaph*, March 24, 1882.

8 *Record-Union*, March 24, 1882.

9 Kate Elder's handwritten notes about her life including her time as Mrs. John Henry Holliday written 1935-1939.

10 https://www.miningfoundationsw.org/resources/documents/publications/history The Old Dominion Copper Mine by Wilbur A. Haak; *Globe, Arizona: The Life and Times of a Western Mining Town, 1864-1917*, 119-121; *Arizona Silver Belt*, May 15, 1882, May 17, 1906.

11 Kate Elder's handwritten notes about her life including her time as Mrs. John Henry Holliday written 1935-1939; *Doc Holliday: A Family Portrait*, 216-217.

12 Kate Elder's handwritten notes about her life including her time as Mrs. John Henry Holliday written 1935-1939.

13 Author Anton Mazzanovich Notes/Interview with Kate Elder June 1932–November 1932; Kate Elder's handwritten notes about her life including her time as Mrs. John Henry Holliday written 1935-1939.

14 Kate Elder's handwritten notes about her life including her time as Mrs. John Henry Holliday written 1935-1939.

15 Ibid.

16 Kate Elder's handwritten notes about her life including her time as Mrs. John Henry Holliday written 1935-1939; *Clifton Clarion*, November 23, 1887; *Daily Sentinel*, November 25, 1887.

17 Kate Elder's handwritten notes about her life including her time as Mrs. John Henry Holliday written 1935-1939.

18 *Helena Independent*, December 14, 1887.

19 Ibid.

20 Kate Elder's handwritten notes about her life including her time as Mrs. John Henry Holliday written 1935-1939.

21 Ibid.

22 Ibid.

23 *Aspen Evening Chronicle*, September 14, 1888.

24 *Carbondale Avalanche*, January 8, 1890.

25 *Carbondale Avalanche*, March 5, 1890; State of Colorado Division of Vital Statistics Marriage Record Report George M. Cummings & Mary K. Horroney, March 2, 1890.

26 Kate Elder's handwritten notes about her life including her time as Mrs. John Henry Holliday written 1935-1939; *Bisbee Daily Review*, October 31, 1908.

27 Kate Elder's handwritten notes about her life including her time as Mrs. John Henry Holliday written 1935-1939.

28 Kate Elder's handwritten notes about her life including her time as Mrs. John Henry Holliday written 1935-1939; *Pueblo Colorado Weekly Chieftan*, May 28, 1896.

29 Kate Elder's handwritten notes about her life including her time as Mrs. John Henry Holliday written 1935-1939; Professor A. W. Bork Notes/Letters/Interview with Kate Elder, Kate's family and friends compiled 1935-1978.

30 Kate Elder's handwritten notes about her life including her time as Mrs. John Henry Holliday written 1935-1939; Professor A. W. Bork Notes/Letters/Interview with Kate Elder, Kate's family and friends compiled 1935-1978; Arizona State Board of Health Death Certificate for George M. Cummings #104.

31 *Fort Wayne Sentinel*, November 4, 1896.

Chapter Eight Life in Dos Cabezas

1 Kate Elder's handwritten letters to Board of Directors of State Institutions written between March 1931 and August 1939; *Cochise County Stalwarts: A Who's Who of the Territorial Years*, vols. 1-2; http://www.waymarking.com/waymarks/WMRKQT Cochise Hotel Cochise, Arizona.

2 Kate Elder's handwritten letters to Board of Directors of State Institutions written between March 1931 and August 1939; http://www.waymarking.com/waymarks/WMRKQT Cochise Hotel Cochise, Arizona; *Tombstone Weekly Epitaph*, February 20, 1882; *When All Roads Led to Tombstone*, 165-166.

3 *Arizona Republican*, September 11, 1899

4 Ibid.

5 Kate Elder's handwritten letters to Board of Directors of State Institutions written between March 1931 and August 1939.

6 Ibid.

7 Ibid.

8 *San Francisco Chronicle*, July 9, 1900.

9 *Arizona Daily Star*, July 14, 1900; Kate Elder's handwritten letters to Board of Directors of State Institutions written between March 1931 and August 1939.

10 Kate Elder's handwritten letters to Board of Directors of State Institutions written between March 1931 and August 1939.

11 Kate Elder's handwritten letters to Board of Directors of State Institutions written between March 1931 and August 1939; Professor A. W. Bork Notes/Letters/Interview with Kate Elder, Kate's family and friends compiled 1935-1978; *The Story of Dos Cabezas*, 15-18.

12 *Arizona Daily Star*, November 1, 1925; www.ancestry.com John J. Howard; 1910 United States Federal Census; *The Story of Dos Cabezas*, 35-43.

13 *Bisbee Daily Review*, February 7, 1907.

14 *The Story of Dos Cabezas*, 35-43.

15 *Arizona Daily Star*, November 11, 1925.

16 *The Story of Dos Cabezas*, 35-43.

17 *Arizona Republican*, April 26, 1906; Kate Elder's handwritten letters to Board of Directors of State Institutions written between March 1931 and August 1939.

18 Kate Elder's handwritten letters to Board of Directors of State Institutions written between March 1931 and August 1939; http://historyoffeminism.com/summary-of-the-social-purity-movement; *Post Standard*, February 8, 1910.

19 www.ancestry.com Mary C Cummings; 1910 United Stated Federal Census.

20 *The Story of Dos Cabezas*, 35-43; Kate Elder's handwritten letters to Board of Directors of State Institutions written between March 1931 and August 1939.

21 Kate Elder's handwritten letters to Board of Directors of State Institutions written between March 1931 and August 1939; *Los Angeles Times*, July 18, 1882.

22 www.ancestry.com Arizona Wills and Probate Records 1803-1995.

23 www.ancestry.com Arizona Wills and Probate Records 1803-1995; Kate Elder's handwritten letters to Board of Directors of State Institutions written between March 1931 and August 1939.

24 *The Story of Dos Cabezas*, 35-43; Kate Elder's handwritten letters to Board of Directors of State Institutions written between March 1931 and August 1939.

25 Ibid.

Chapter Nine The Pioneers' Home

1 Kate Elder's handwritten letters to Governor George Hunt written between January 1931 to July 1937 and Governor Hunt's response.

2 Kate Elder's handwritten notes about her life including her time as Mrs. John Henry Holliday written 1935-1939.

3 Kate Elder's handwritten letters to Board of Directors of State Institutions written between March 1931 and August 1939 and the response from Board of Directors of State Institutions.

4 Ibid.

5 https://www.nationalregisterofhistoricplaces.com/az/Yavapai/state.html; *Arizona Daily Star*, September 21, 1930; *Arizona Republican*, December 30, 1929.

6 Kate Elder's handwritten letters to Board of Directors of State Institutions written between March 1931 and August 1939 and the response from Board of Directors of State Institutions.

7 Ibid.

8 Ibid.

9 *Arizona Daily Star*, December 26, 1931.

10 *Arizona Daily Star*, June 12, 1932, October 2, 1932.

11 Kate Elder's handwritten letters to Board of Directors of State Institutions written between March 1931 and August 1939 and the response from Board of Directors of State Institutions.

12 Kate Elder's handwritten letters to Board of Directors of State Institutions written between March 1931 and August 1939 and the response from Board of Directors of State Institutions.

13 Kate Elder's handwritten letters to Governor Baker Moeur written 1935-1936.

14 Response to Kate Elder's letter to Governor Moeur from Arthur N. Kelley, Board of Directors of State Institutions.

15 Kate Elder's letter to Arthur N. Kelley, Board of Directors of State Institutions.

16 Response to Kate Elder's letter to Arthur N. Kelley, Board of Directors of State Institutions.

17 Kate Elder's handwritten notes about her life including her time as Mrs. John Henry Holliday written 1935-1939; author Anton Mazzanovich Notes/Interview with Kate Elder June 1932–November 1932; Professor A. W. Bork Notes/Letters/Interview with Kate Elder, Kate's family and friends compiled 1935-1978; Kate Elder's letters to her niece Lillian Lane Rafferty written between May 1935 and March 1940.

18 *Arizona Republic*, November 5, 1940; *Tucson Daily Citizen*, November 4, 1940; Arizona State Board of Health Death Certificate for Mary K. Cummings #421.

19 Kate Elder's letters to her niece Lillian Lane Rafferty written between May 1935 and March 1940.

Chapter Ten The Legend of Kate Elder

1 *Wyatt Earp: Frontier Marshal*, 197-198.

2 Author Anton Mazzanovich Notes/Interview with Kate Elder June 1932–November 1932.

3 *Family, Friends and Foes*, vol. 1, 13-14.

4 *San Francisco Examiner*, March 15, 1942.

5 *On Borrowed Time*, 18-21.

6 *Los Angeles Times*, December 14, 1946; *Denton Record-Chronicle*, November 17, 1946.

7 *Battle Creek Enquirer*, June 23, 1957.

8 *Shamokin News-Dispatch*, June 1, 1953.

9 *Boston Globe*, August 5, 1971.

10 *Montgomery Advertiser*, December 28, 1993.

11 www.rogerebert.com/revews/wyattearp1994.

12 *The Filmgoers' Guide to the Great Westerns: Stagecoach to Tombstone*, 150-152.

13 *The Gazette*, August 12, 1939.

14 Ibid.

15 Kate Elder's handwritten notes about her life including her time as Mrs. John Henry Holliday written 1935-1939; Kate Elder's letters to her niece Lillian Lane Rafferty written between May 1935 and March 1940.

16 *San Francisco Examiner*, March 15, 1942; *American Weekly*, December 8, 1948; *Brownsville Herald*, November 26, 1946.

17 *Shamokin News-Dispatch*, April 20, 1946.

Bibliography

General Sources

Abbott, Karen. *Sin in the Second City: Madams, Ministers, Playboys, and the Battle for America's Soul*. New York: Random House, 2008.

Agnew, Jeremy. *The Old West in Fact in Film: History Versus Hollywood Jefferson*. Jefferson, NC: McFarland, 2012.

Aikman, Duncan. *Calamity Jane and the Lady Wildcats*. Lincoln: University of Nebraska, 1927.

Bailey, Lynn R., and Chaput, Don. *Cochise County Stalwarts: A Who's Who of the Territorial Years*, vols. 1-2. Tucson, AZ: Westernlore, 2000.

Barra, Allen. *Inventing Wyatt Earp*. New York: Carroll & Graf, 1998.

Bigando, Robert. *Globe, Arizona: The Life and Times of a Western Mining Town, 1864-1917*. Globe, AZ: Mountain Spirit Press, 1990.

Boyer, Glenn G. *I Married Wyatt Earp: The Recollections of Josephine Sarah Marcus Earp*. Stamford, CT: Longmeadow Press, 1994.

Boyer, Glenn G. *Wyatt Earp: Family, Friends and Foes*, vol. 1. "Who Was Big Nose Kate?"

Braddock, Betty, and Covalt, Jeanie. *Dodge City: Cowboy Capital*. Dodge City, KS: Kansas Heritage Center, 1982.

Burns, Walter Noble. *Tombstone*. New York: Grosset & Dunlap, 1929.

Carlson, Bruce. *Some Awfully Tame, but Kinda Funny Stories about Early Missouri Ladies-of-the-Evening*. Sioux City, IA: Quixote Press, 1991.

Carter, Samuel III. *Cowboy Capital of the World: The Saga of Dodge City*. New York: Doubleday, 1973.

Coleman, Candia Jane. *Doc Holliday's Woman*. New York: Warner Books, 1995.

Cooper, David K. C. *Doctors of Another Calling: Physicians Who Are Known Best in Fields Other than Medicine*. Newark: University of Delaware Press, 2015.

de la Garza, Phyllis. *The Story of Dos Cabezas*. Tucson, AZ: Westernlore Press, 1995.

DeArment, Robert K. *Bat Masterson: The Man and the Legend*. Norman: University of Oklahoma Press, 1979

Dobak, William A., and Phillips, Thomas D. *The Black Regulars, 1866-1898*. Norman: University of Oklahoma Press, 2017.

Enss, Chris. *Love Untamed: Romances of the Old West*. Guilford, CT: TwoDot Books, 2002.

Enss, Chris. *Wicked Women: Notorious, Mischievous, and Wayward Ladies from the Old West*. Guilford, CT: TwoDot Books, 2015.

Enss, Chris, and Kazanjian, Howard. *Thunder over the Prairie: The True Story of a Murder and a Manhunt by the Greatest Posse of All Time*. Guilford, CT: TwoDot Books, 2009.

Gray, John Pleasant. *When All Roads Led to Tombstone*. Boise, ID: Tamarack Books, 1998.

Hickey, Michael M. *Street Fight in Tombstone, Near the OK*. Honolulu, HI: Corral Talei, 1991.

Hughes, Howard. *The Filmgoers' Guide to the Great Westerns: Stagecoach to Tombstone*. New York: I. B. Tauris, 2008.

Hunter, Julius K. *Priscilla & Babe: From Slavery's Shackles to Millionaire Bordello Madams in Victorian Saint Louis*. Saint Louis, MO: Bluebird, 2014.

Jahns, Pat. *The Frontier World of Doc Holliday*. New York: Indian Head Books, 1957.

Kimkris, Jackling. On Borrowed Time. Tucson, AZ: Youradaisy Press, 2016.

Lake, Stuart N. *Wyatt Earp: Frontier Marshal*. New York: Pocket Books, 1931.

MacKell, Jan. *Brothels, Bordellos, and Bad Girls: Prostitution in Colorado 1860-1930*. Albuquerque: University of New Mexico Press, 2004.

Masterson, William B. *Famous Gunfighters of the Western Frontier*. Houston, TX: Frontier Press 1907.

Meyers, John M. *Doc Holliday*. Lincoln: University of Nebraska Press, 1973.

Parkhill, Forbes. *The Wildest of the West*. New York: Henry Holt, 1951.

Reavis, Logan Uriah. *Saint Louis: The Future Great City of the World*. St. Louis, MO: Gray, Baker, 1875.

Roberts, Gary L. *Doc Holliday: The Life and Legend*. Hoboken, NJ: John Wiley, 2006.

Russell, Thaddeus. *Renegade History of the United States*. New York: Free Press, 2011.

Selcer, Richard F. *Hell's Half Acre*. Fort Worth: Texas Christian University Press, 1991.

Tanner, Karen *Holliday. A Family Portrait*. Norman: University of Oklahoma Press, 1998.

Tefertiller, Casey. *Wyatt Earp: The Life behind the Legend*. New York: John Wiley, 1997.

Vestal, Stanley. *Dodge City: Queen of Cowtowns*. New York: Pennant Books, 1952.

Young, Fredric R. *Dodge City: Up through a Century in Story and Pictures*. Dodge City, KS: Boot Hill Museum, 1972.

Correspondence

Email exchange between Chris Enss and Sr. Thomas More Daley, OSU archivist, Ursuline Archives, Central Province, USA. Emails dated December 20, 2017, January 17, 2019, February 27, 2018, and February 28, 2018.

Letter written in January 1869 by Mary May, also known as Mary Horony, authorizing attorney Otto Smith to give her portion of her inheritance from deceased parents to her brothers and sisters.

Scott County Court, Reel #87 (vol. 7, p. 163), May 1865, In the Matter of the Estate of Dr. Michael Harony, deceased.

Scott County Court, Reel #101, 1865, Report of Otto Smith, re: Harony minors and probate record.

Magazines/Periodicals

Arizona Journal of Arizona History, vol. 26, no. 4, winter 1985. "The Women Was Too Tough," Virginia Culin Roberts.

Arizona and the West, vol. 19, no.1, spring 1977. "O.K. Corral Fight at Tombstone: A Footnote by Kate Elder," edited by A. W. Bork & Glenn Boyer.

Kanhistique Journal, Kansas Historical Society, summer 2006.
Kansas History Journal, vol. 2, spring 1977. "Wyatt Earp, Family & Foes in 1877."
Kansas History Journal, vol. 2, no. 1, spring 1979. "Prostitution and Changing Morality in the Frontier Cattle Towns of Kansas," Carol Leonard and Isidor Wallimann.
Prologue: *Quarterly of National Archives*. "Bridging the Mississippi: The Railroads and Steamboats Clash at the Rock Island Bridge," David A. Pfeiffer.
Real West Magazine, vol. 24, no. 175, March 1981.
Saga: True Adventures for Men, March 1961. "Authentic Life Story: Doc Holliday: The West's Greatest Gunman," John Myers.
True Frontier Magazine, April 1972.
True West Magazine, November 1992.
True West Magazine, May 1999. "Wyatt Earp and Doc Holliday in Las Vegas, New Mexico," Chuck Hornung.
True West Magazine, November/December 2001.
Voyage to the United States, vol. 3, chapter XXIV. "From San Antonio to Eagle Pass," Guillermo Prieto, 1818-1897.
Wild West Magazine, vol. 29, no. 3, October 2016.

Miscellaneous

Arizona State Board of Health Death Certificate for George M. Cummings #104.
Arizona State Board of Health Death Certificate for Mary K. Cummings #421.
Arizona Territorial Census Records, 1864-1882.
Arrest/Court Records, Ford County, Kansas, Bessie Earp and Sallie Earp, September 15, 1874.
Author Anton Mazzanovich Notes/Interview with Kate Elder, June 1932–November 1932.
Author Glenn Boyer Notes/Letters/Interview with A. W. Bork, Mark K. Cummings family and friends, compiled 1973-1996.
Cochise County the Territory of Arizona vs. John H. Holliday Criminal Register of Actions, Case #23.
Cochise County the Territory of Arizona vs. John H. Holliday Criminal Register of Actions, Case #30.
"Cultural Intersections and Historic Preservation: A Study of Las Vegas, New Mexico," Eileen Vanessa Rojas. Thesis in Historic Preservation for the University of Pennsylvania, 1998.
Dodge City Ordinances, no. 41 and no. 42, Dodge City Manual, 1878.
Ford County Historical Society research paper, "Girls of the Golden West," Joseph Snell, 1964.
Kansas Census Records, 1864-1885.
Kate Elder's handwritten notes about her life, including her time as Mrs. John Henry Holliday, written 1935-1939.
Kate Elder's handwritten letters to Governor George Hunt written between January 1931 to July 1937 and the response from Governor Hunt.

Kate Elder's handwritten letters to Governor Baker Moeur written 1935 to 1936 and the response from Governor Moeur.

Kate Elder's handwritten letters to Board of Directors of State Institutions written between March 1931 to August 1939 and the response from Board of Directors of State Institutions.

Kate Elder's letters to her niece Lillian Lane Rafferty written between May 1935 to March 1940.

Land Claims #1, Cochise County, J. J. Howard, April 30, 1879.

Missouri Census Records, 1865-1895.

Naturalization Index, Scott County, Iowa, 1842-1930.

New York, Passenger and Crew List, 1820-1957, National Archives.

O.K. Corral Inquest, November 1881.

Professor A. W. Bork Notes/Letters/Interview with Kate Elder, Kate's family and friends, compiled 1935-1978.

San Miguel County, New Mexico Deed of Records, 1875-1885.

San Miguel County, New Mexico Territory Criminal Record Book, 1876-1879.

State of Colorado Division of Vital Statistics, Marriage Record Report, George M. Cummings and Mary K. Horony, March 2, 1940.

Wichita City Records, Misc. Papers, 1874.

Newspapers

Abilene Reporter, Abilene, Texas, September 22, 1971

Albuquerque Journal, Albuquerque, New Mexico, March 11, 2003

American Weekly, New York, December 8, 1948

Arizona Daily Star, Tucson, Arizona, July 14, 1900; April 22, 1908; April 8, 1911; November 1, 1925; November 11, 1925; September 21, 1930; September 17, 1931; December 26, 1931; June 12, 1932; October 2, 1932

Arizona Republican, Phoenix, Arizona, November 5, 1940; March 29, 1898; September 11, 1899; August 7, 1902; April 19, 1903; April 26, 1906; April 3, 1907; December 30, 1929; January 23, 2000

Arizona Silver Belt, Globe, Arizona, May 15, 1882; June 23, 1888; May 17, 1906; May 7, 1909; June 15, 1915

Arizona Weekly Citizen, Tucson, Arizona, March 24, 1881; August 28, 1881; November 13, 1881; May 15, 1882; July 4, 1891

Arizona Weekly Star, Tucson, Arizona, March 31, 1881

Aspen Daily Times, Aspen, Colorado, November 9, 1887

Aspen Evening Chronicle, Aspen, Colorado, September 14, 1888; May 30, 1889

Aspen Rocky Mountain Sun, Aspen, Colorado, June 10, 1882; July 14, 1888; July 21, 1888

Aspen Weekly Chronicle, Aspen, Colorado, January 1, 1889

Atchison Champion, Atchison, Kansas, April 9, 1875

Atchison Daily Champion, Atchison, Kansas, April 9, 1875; August 7, 1875; August 22, 1875; June 25, 1878

Austin American-Statesman, Austin, Texas, February 21, 1877; January 31, 1963

Battle Creek Enquirer, Battle Creek, Michigan, June 23, 1957; September 21, 1900; October 3, 1902; January 13, 1903; February 7, 1907; October 31, 1908; August 17, 1909

Bismarck Tribune, Bismarck, North Dakota, March 12, 1951

Boston Globe, Boston, Massachusetts, August 5, 1971

Brewery Gulch Gazette, Bisbee, Arizona, June 3, 1932

Brownsville Herald, Brownsville, Texas, November 26, 1946

Carbondale Avalanche, Carbondale, Colorado, January 1, 1890; January 8, 1890; March 5, 1890; October 1, 1890; November 20, 1891; July 1, 1896; July 1, 1897

Chase County Leader, Cottonwood Falls, Kansas, July 10, 1875

Chicago Tribune, Chicago, Illinois, July 31, 1870

Cincinnati Enquirer, Cincinnati, Ohio, April 4, 1878

Clifton Clarion, Clifton, Arizona, November 23, 1887

Daily Commonwealth, Topeka, Kansas, February 26, 1876

Daily Gazette, Las Vegas, New Mexico, September 30, 1878; November 6, 1879

Daily Republican, Monongahela, Pennsylvania, August 16, 1935

Daily Sentinel, Garden City, Kansas, November 25, 1882

Dallas Daily Herald, Dallas, Texas, January 11, 1878

Davenport Daily Gazette, Davenport, Iowa, April 29, 1865

Denton Record-Chronicle, Denton, Texas, November 17, 1946

Detroit Free Press, Detroit, Michigan, July 14, 1870; May 29, 1878; June 29, 1878; July 13, 1878; July 20, 1878; July 27, 1878; August 10, 1878; August 13, 1878; August 17, 1878; December 12, 1878; March 9, 1879

Evening Star, Washington, DC, February 9, 1878

Florence Tribune, Florence, Arizona, October 6, 1900

Fort Wayne Sentinel, Fort Wayne, Indiana, November 4, 1896

Galveston Daily News, Galveston, Texas, May 21, 1878; August 23, 1877

Gazette, Iowa City, Iowa, August 12, 1939

Globe Republican, Dodge City, Kansas, August 20, 1878

Graham Guardian, Safford, Arizona, June 16, 1911

Great Bend Register, Great Bend, Kansas, July 9, 1874; August 20, 1874; November 19, 1874

Green-Bay Press-Gazette, Green Bay, Wisconsin, February 2, 1992

Helena Independent, Helena, Montana, December 14, 1887

Hold County Sentinel, Oregon, Missouri, June 26, 1868

Kansas Free State, Lawrence, Kansas, April 14, 1855

Las Vegas Gazette, Las Vegas, New Mexico, March 23, 1879; April 14, 1879; July 29, 1879; September 14, 1879; February 10, 1880

Las Vegas Optic, Las Vegas, New Mexico, July 20, 1881; December 16, 1898

Leavenworth Times, Leavenworth, Kansas, October 31, 1875

Leavenworth Weekly Times, Leavenworth, Kansas, November 24, 1870

Lincoln County Herald, Troy, Missouri, June 1, 1856

Logansport Pharos-Tribune, Logansport, Indiana, November 1, 1896

Los Angeles Times, Los Angeles, California, July 18, 1882; December 14, 1946

Macon Republican, Macon, Missouri, August 29, 1872
Marshall Messenger, Marshall, Texas, January 10, 1879
Montgomery Advertiser, Montgomery, Alabama, December 28, 1993
Newton Kansan, Newton, Kansas, August 19, 1875
New York Times, New York, October 15, 1866; November 16, 2007
New York Tribune, New York, March 21, 1872
Osage County Chronicle, Burlingame, Kansas, August 24, 1876
Parsons Weekly Sun, Parsons, Kansas, July 20, 1878
Post Standard, Syracuse, New York, February 8, 1910
Prescott Courier, Prescott, Arizona, December 26, 1993
Pueblo Colorado Weekly Chiefton, Pueblo, Colorado, May 28, 1896
Quad-City Times, Davenport, Iowa, September 16, 1990
Record-Union, Sacramento, California, March 17, 1881; March 24, 1882
Rochester Daily Union, Rochester, New York, October 10, 1866
San Francisco Chronicle, San Francisco, California, July 9, 1900
San Francisco Examiner, San Francisco, California, August 2, 1896; March 15, 1942
Shamokin News-Dispatch, Shamokin, Pennsylvania, April 20, 1946; June 1, 1953
St. Louis Post Dispatch, St. Louis, Missouri, March 3, 1874
St. Louis Weekly Democrat, St. Louis, Missouri, February 6, 1872
State Journal, Frankfurt, Kentucky, March 6, 1874
Taloga Star, Taloga, Kansas, May 25, 1888
Tombstone Epitaph, Tombstone, Arizona, March 24, 1882
Tombstone Weekly Epitaph, Tombstone, Arizona, February 20, 1882; March 26, 1911
Tri-Weekly Examiner, Atlanta, Georgia, August 6, 1869
Tri-Weekly Herald, Marshall, Texas, October 15, 1878; October 19, 1878; May 13, 1878
Tucson Citizen, Tucson, Arizona, March 21, 1882; June 6, 1964
Tucson Daily Citizen, Tucson, Arizona, November 4, 1940
Weekly Arizona Miner, Prescott, Arizona, March 12, 1880; April 2, 1880; April 9, 1880
Weekly Arizona Republican, Phoenix, Arizona, April 26, 1906
Weekly Atchison Champion, Atchison, Kansas, August 14, 1875
Weekly Caucasian, Lexington, Missouri, August 13, 1870; January 27, 1872
Weekly Commonwealth, Topeka, Kansas, September 9, 1875
Weekly Journal Miner, Prescott, Arizona, September 26, 1900
Weekly New Mexican, Santa Fe, New Mexico, January 11, 1879
Wichita Daily Eagle, Wichita, Kansas, August 10, 1871; May 28, 1873; July 15, 1874
Wichita Weekly Eagle, Wichita, Kansas, June 21, 1873; July 19, 1873; January 8, 1874;
    August 2, 1874
Winchester Argus, Winchester, Kansas, May 2, 1878
Winfield Courier, Winfield, Kansas, May 30, 1878

Websites
www.ancestry.com Arizona Wills and Probate Records 1803-1995
www.ancestry.com Iowa, Wills and Probate Records, 1758-1997
www.ancestry.com John J. Howard 1910 United States Federal Census

www.ancestry.com Mary Katherine Horony

www.ancestry.com Mary C. Cummings 1910 United Stated Federal Census

www.britannica.com/biography/Maximilian-archduke-of-Austria-and-emperor
   -of-Mexico

http://cochisehotel.net/about-us.html

https://devnewmexicohistory.org

www.everyculture.com/multi/Ha-La/Hungarian-Americans.html

https://genealogy.mohistory.org/genealogy/name/163167?a=1

http://genealogy.mohistory.org/geneology/name/161167?a=1

www.history.com/news/the-disease-that-helped-put-colorado-on-the-map

http://historyoffeminism.com/summary-of-the-social-purity-movement

https://history-ray's place.com/ks/se-wichita-early.htm

www.legendsofamerica.com/nm-lasvegas

https://mainstreetlvnm.org/home/history-of-las-vegas

www.miningfoundationsw.org/resources/documents/publications/history The Old
   Dominion Copper Mine by Wilbur A. Haak

www.nationalregisterofhistoricplaces.com/az/Yavapai/state.html

www.rogerebert.com/reviews/wyattearp1994

www.sciencedirect.com/science/article/pii/S095461110600401X

www.slate.com/blogs/thevault

www.smithsonianmag.com/science-nature/how-tuberculosis-shaped-victorian-fashion
   -180959029

https://stlouis-mo.gov/government/department

www.stltoday.com/entertainment/books-and-literature/q-a-doc-holliday-s
   -summer

www.texasbeyondhistory.net/forts/griffin/index.html

https://tshaonline.org/handbook/online/articles/exj01

https://tshaonline.org/handbook/online/articles/hlm77 Mobeetie, Texas

https://tucson.com/news/local/congress-st-name-honors-tucson-saloon/article
   _8668z9aaa-ae

www.waymarking.com/waymarks/WMRKQT Cochise Hotel Cochise, Arizona

www.worldportsource.com Port of Bremen, Germany

Index

About the Author

Chris Enss is a *New York Times* best-selling author who has been writing about women of the Old West for more than twenty years. She has penned more than forty published books on the subject. Her book entitled *Entertaining Ladies: Actresses, Singers, and Dancers in the Old West* was a Spur Award finalist in 2017. Enss's book *Mochi's War: The Tragedy of the Sand Creek Massacre* received the Will Rogers Medallion Award for best nonfiction Western for 2015. Her book entitled *Object Matrimony: The Risky Business of Mail Order Matchmaking on the Western Frontier* won the Elmer Kelton Award for Best Nonfiction book of 2013. Enss's book *Sam Sixkiller: Frontier Cherokee Lawman* was named Outstanding Book on Oklahoma History by the Oklahoma Historical Society. She received the Spirit of the West Alive award, cosponsored by the Wild West Gazette, celebrating her efforts to keep the spirit of the Old West alive for future generations, and the Citizen of the Year Award from the Nevada County Historical Society for preserving the history of the Gold Country and the West.